73

Glitter in the Blood

A Poet's Manifesto for Better, Braver Writing

ᑕᔓ

by Mindy Nettifee

Write Bloody Publishing
America's Independent Press

Austin, TX

WRITEBLOODY.COM

Nettifee, Mindy.
1ˢᵗ edition.
ISBN: 978-1-938912-01-6

Interior Layout by Lea C. Deschenes
Cover Designed by Gary
Author Photo by Brian S. Ellis
Interior Illustrations by Mindy Nettifee
Proofread by Ronnie K. Stephens
Edited by Derrick Brown
Type set in Bergamo from www.theleagueofmoveabletype.com

Other books by Mindy Nettifee:
Rise of the Trust Fall, Write Bloody Publishing
Sleepyhead Assassins, Moon Tide Press

Printed in Tennessee, USA

Write Bloody Publishing
Austin, TX
Support Independent Presses
writebloody.com

To contact the author, send an email to writebloody@gmail.com

MADE IN THE USA

GLITTER IN THE BLOOD

Glitter in the Blood

IN CONCLUSION

THE AUTHOR'S FORWARD

The first title I imagined for this book was *Glitter In The Blood: A Poet's Manifesto For Better, Braver Writing and Living*. That tail needed to be cut off. However, it is a central belief of mine that how you do anything is how you do everything. I think some yogi high on Topanga Canyon oxygen said that to me once. It stuck. It rearranged me.

I am not sure I can write about how I write without writing about how I live. I am not sure I can share with you the rules and unrules that govern my creative process without revealing to you how I dream at night, how I cook my soup on Sundays, how I have lived through what I've lived through and wrestled sanity and integrity from it, while also reminding myself daily as an artist and a human that, in the words of choreographer Pina Bausch, "You just have to get crazier."

But let's stay unfocused shall we? The central thesis of this poetry manifesto is about bravery. Once, after just having done the soul-shatteringest, scariest, bravest thing I had done to date, I walked out into the November night shaking and called a friend. I said, "I did the math. I KNOW know this is what I was supposed to do. So why do I feel like a monster?" The friend said, "Oh. That's what being brave feels like. That's why so many people never do it."

A month earlier, I had gone to the big shmanzy Hollywood premiere screening of Danny Boyle's film *127 Hours*, in support of a friend who had been in the movie. I knew nothing about the movie going in. If you haven't seen it, you will not understand when I tell you that the first hour of it was one of the most unbearable of my life. James Franco's portrayal of canyoneer Aron Ralston, who was trapped in an isolated canyon in Utah when his arm became pinned down by a boulder, and who eventually had to cut his own arm off to save his life, was a little *too good*. As Aron got hungrier and thirstier and more desperate, I became hungrier and thirstier and more desperate. When he finally resolved to sever his arm and began, I could barely watch. These high-pitched chaotic strings played to represent the cutting of the nerves. I tried not to throw up. But he does it! He *did* it! And he emerged from the crevice, stumbled and fell to a dirty shallow pool of rainwater to drink, and then miraculously found hikers, rescuers. The ending was one of the most triumphant, emotional moments possible in cinema. But wait! This is not a too-long paragraph about that movie, but what happened after the standing ovation, and after the audience sat back down, openly sobbing, in shock. A man in the row in front of me stood up and began to make his way to the aisle. He was missing an arm. It was Aron. He walked up to the stage and was given a microphone, and made a brief, humbling, unaffected speech. He told us he was grateful for his experience, because what we need more than anything else in this world is stories of survival. He challenged us all to think about the boulders in our lives. He challenged us to get free of them, whatever it takes.

What I want to challenge you to do while reading this book and after, is to continue on your path as a human and a writer to be braver and braver and braver. This means doing "the work." This means following your fear as often as you follow your happiness. "The work" is about personal growth, about exploring the unlit recesses in yourself that may or may not yield to your research.[1] Doing "the work" means digging so deep you can no longer see the light. It means writing about the things that have such an emotional charge for you, you avoid thinking about them, let alone writing about them. And let me be clear—when I say "emotional charge," I do not just mean the sharp sparks of fear or shame, though those emotions are clear indications of something you need to confront. I also mean fear and shame's younger sister, embarrassment. I also mean anger and rage. I also mean sadness. I also mean despair, and despair's twin, elation.

I am challenging you to do this because this is what I challenge myself to do— to use my writing as a tool to free myself of the boulders. To madly engage in the process of living. To allow myself to be changed by my life experiences and my writing. To let go of my expectations, the ones I have even when I think I don't, of what I will be like on the other side of that change. To grow and grow and grow. To become whatever it is I am supposed to become.

In addition to honing in on my general tone and intent for this book, you may as well get used to me quoting Rob Brezsny, and other members of the radical intelligentsia, right now. He once wrote:

> It's a great privilege to live in a free country. You're fortunate if you have the opportunity to pursue your dreams without having to ward off government interference or corporate brainwashing or religious fanaticism.

> But that's only partly useful if you have not yet won the most important struggle for liberation, which is the freedom from your own unconscious obsessions and conditioned responses. Becoming an independent agent who's not an unwitting slave to his or her shadow is one of the most heroic feats a human can accomplish.[2]

This book *is* a guide to writing poetry. It contains practical advice about how to begin poems and end poems, how to play with structure, invent fresher imagery, make your poems tighter and more meaningful in the way you want them to be. But this is also a book where we enter sacred ground together—

our imaginations, our inner emotional geography, our shadow selves. We are doing this in order to become better writers, yes, but also to attempt the greater mastery that Brezsny gauntlets. *How you do anything is how you do everything.*

It is never too early in the day to be swallowing that kind of medicine.

There is one more thing I have to say about why I'm declaring a collective poet journey into the inner unknown. Carl Jung believed that, "in spite of its function as a reservoir for human darkness—or perhaps because of this—the shadow is the seat of creativity."[3] Regardless of what you discover in the process of reading this book and doing the work it asks of you, you are headed straight to the center of the creativity engines. Its constantly shifting architecture is built by the cumulative wealth of everything you have ever seen or heard or felt or wished. It's where the worst nightmare you have ever had and your most beautiful Seuss-on-dopamine dream both came from.

If you're not afraid of those hidden inner clockworks, of what you'll find in the dark, you're not not paying attention. But bravery is not about lacking fear; it's about being scared out of your mind and still taking the plunge. I'm ready if you're ready.

IN THE BEGINNING

"The moment of change is the only poem."
—Adrienne Rich

CHAPTER 1: THE MYTH OF INSPIRATION

Most of us start writing poetry because of the lightning bolts of emotion coursing through us that we are desperate to translate into thunder. It is not a completely unfair generalization to say that poets typically begin writing in "confessional mode," later move on to a deeper and weirder mode of exploring language, syntax, metaphor and abstraction, and then even later move on to playing with a synthesis of the two. Of course this is not true of all writers. Especially those first introduced to poetry through stream-of-consciousness visionaries like Jack Kerouac or master subversives like Gertrude Stein. But let's all take a moment and remember what first moved us to write poetry.

For me, it was the need to claw my way out of a crippling adolescent depression, the kind so severe and existentially confusing it led to ill-informed suicide attempts with bottles of Motrin IB. I was twelve. I survived my third attempt at ending my young life by puking pretty hard and very pink, and looking up to notice the brand name tattooed in elegant grey on the toilet seat: *Church*. Being a preacher's daughter—and more specifically, the daughter of a gay genius preacher who struggled with mental illness following the trauma of coming out and losing his family and, well, everything—this simple word being introduced to my prostrate situation made me laugh. Hysterically, maybe, but also genuinely and gently. Right then the seed of something powerful and healing was planted in me. A word and its multiple, simultaneous meanings had changed me.

Not too long after, I "acquired" an old paperback Norton Anthology of Poetry. I *may* have stolen it from a Sunday School library. It was the one with the yolk yellow cover and vaguely Greco-Roman art. The pages smelled like basement, or tornado, and were not uniformly loved. Chaucer was crisp as brand new bibles; Berryman was dog-eared and smudged. I liked how heavy it was. I liked the difficult words. I liked how reading some of the poems aloud was like chewing leather.

Mostly, I liked the way none of it made sense to me. It made the book feel stolen in more than one way. It was like a chronicle of ancient mysterious secrets had fallen into my possession. It was all written in impossible code. Learning to understand it, I knew, meant learning a foreign language, maybe several. There were things in this book that I was not supposed to know, I was sure of it–why else would it be written so strangely? Surely, I thought, if I studied it long enough, everything there was to know about life would be revealed to me.

Adorable. Anyway, that was that. I began writing terrible poetry. Tons of it.

★ ★ ★

For the next fifteen years, I was a fierce and fraught adherent to the "Inspiration" model of writing. I only wrote when something inside me had begun scratching at my surfaces, when some story or emotion had me by the throat. I attended open mics religiously (pun intended) and worried desperately about Writer's Block, the great nemesis of creativity.

But then I started to notice something. Though for weeks and often months I would be suffering from the big WB, the moment a feature booking or project deadline was imminent, my deep fear of not impressing this group of scary-smart, super-free poets I had grown to fiercely admire and love with "New Work" started the adrenaline engines pumping. And magically, I was unblocked.

I also happened upon these two gems of advice. Maybe you've heard or read them before. The first is from poet Kay Ryan, who describes her writing process as, "'a self-imposed emergency,' the artistic equivalent of finding a loved one pinned under a 3,000-pound car. These 'emergencies,' she says, allow her to tap into abilities she wouldn't normally have, much like a father who single-handedly lifts a vehicle off his child."[4] The second gem came from the brilliant mind of Edward James Olmos. If I remember correctly (and I rarely do), he was giving a speech at UCLA. He said something about how it was easy to learn to have the discipline to do the things we have to do. What was infinitely harder was the opposite. He said, and this is a direct quote, "Now I also discipline myself to do things I love to do when I don't want to do them." So say we all.

I began experimenting with inventing emergencies, and with bringing some kind of discipline to doing the thing that I loved—writing poetry. This isn't to say that this new process I was exploring wasn't a form of inspiration. Or that inspiration isn't something you can cultivate in yourself as an attitude or behavior, like curiosity, or better dental hygiene. But I knew if I wanted to write, and to keep writing better and better poems, then it was time to stop waiting for lightning to strike.

Let me boil down my epiphany of how I thought this "disciplining" oneself was going to work into three basic and over-simplified steps. I will underscore this boiling down by changing from narrative tone to direct address:

STEP ONE: Read more poetry. I cannot emphasize this enough. Get thee to the interwebs, or a local library, or a quiet corner of a Barnes & Noble.

(Trust: the poetry section of a Barnes & Noble is guaranteed to be a quiet corner.) Read and read and read. Read until you find something you love so much, it makes you want to quit writing because [insert poet's name here] just said what you've always been burning to say better than you'll ever be able to say it. Then keep reading until you find another, and another.

STEP TWO: Study the poems you love. The magic infuriating gorgeous poems you found by diligently practicing step one? Collect these poems like talismans. Return to them over and over. Study them. Ask yourself why you love them so much. Ask the poems how they work. Try to understand their alchemy. What is it about the beginning that draws you in? What words and phrases gut you? When and where and how did they arrive? Pretend the poem is a land you are discovering for the first time and make a map of it. Or pretend the poem is a text book, and it's your job to come up with its table of contents. Or pretend the poem is the best cake you've ever eaten, but its recipe is lost and you need to reinvent it. Do whatever you want, but these poems are the best teachers you are ever going to get.

STEP THREE: Write more poetry. I'll get to some specific suggestions about how exactly to go about that in the next chapters. But work begets work. I think Brion James said that, and he was spot on. Work begets work, and writing begets writing. Imagine writing as a muscle that you need to use, maybe daily, but at least several times a week so that it gets stronger, so that more blood flows to it. You need the blood flow. If there is no blood flow, there can be no glitter.

ASSIGNMENT

1. Design a plan for systematically reading more poetry.

Decide you are going to discover a new poet every week, or read 4 books of poetry a month. You need a concrete challenge with numbers. And then you need to get your scavenger hunt on. Some tips:

- Anthologies are great places to start. You get introduced to a ton of new-to-you poets all at once. Some of my favorites over the years have been the annual *Pushcart Prize – Best of the Small Presses* anthologies. Or the McSweeny's brilliant *Poets Picking Other Poets*. Or *Billy Collins' 180* books he edited when he was Poet Laureate. Or *The Outlaw Bible To American Poetry*.

- The same can be said of poetry journals and magazines, many of which are available online. Poetrysociety.org has an exhaustive list. There are ones that have been around for decades, and new ones cropping up every year. You will discover pretty quickly that you hate some of them; they aren't your taste at all. But when you discover ones you love—bingo.

- Look up major poetry awards and see who has won them, and then seek out their work.

- Go to MFA program websites. On some of them you can look up their classes and required reading lists, which will introduce you to all kinds of poems you love and hate.

- Ask your trusted poet friends to give you their Top Five Desert Island poets lists.

- The Poetry Foundation has a great online resource where you can look up poems by subject or author. And Poets & Writers has a catalogue of poets from around the country. Get list-y.

- All of this does not mean you need to start spending thousands of dollars a year buying books. Your new best friend is your local library. Did you know you can ask your local library to get books for you?

2. Start a collection of your favorite poems by other people.

I have a folder on my computer called "OPP" that I have been keeping and updating for about a decade. I know another writer who has a crappy leather briefcase filled with them. Every time you find a poem you love, save it somehow.

3. Set aside time every day to write.

You will have days, yes, where life and work and crises and feelings and obligations feel like impossible obstacles to making this happen. And you will not wither and die as a writer if you go through periods where you do not write, but just live. But something happens to me if I go too long without writing. It's a sort of spiritual constipation. There's no other less-gross way to describe it. And going back to a daily practice of writing rids me of this haunting feeling of being stuck and blocked. When I am not travelling an insane schedule like a mentally-ill Monarch Butterfly, I write every morning while drinking my first cup of coffee, before the day has had a chance to sweep me into emailing and working and whatever. Sometimes I only get in 30 minutes. Sometimes it ends up not being writing at all, but some bizarre other creative instinct takes over me and I decide I need to get out the glue sticks and dinosaur figurines. Sometimes I end up writing for hours.

CHAPTER 2: BEGIN ANYWHERE

It was composer John Cage who said that, when commenting on what to do about creative paralysis. John Cage was an American composer dedicated to the application of Zen philosophy to his life, his music, his writing and his lectures. He was so intense, he made even Alan Watts bristle. He might be most famous for his collection titled *Silence*. A musical composer naming his book *Silence* should tell you everything you need to know about John Cage. But Dadaism and I digress.

"Begin anywhere" is fantastic advice. Notice how I keep quoting other thinkers? That's because that's where a lot of my ideas come from. And it's where a lot of your ideas come from. There is not only nothing new under the sun, there is nothing new under the moon, the stars, the Icarus metaphors, or the bone similes. Copy?

This is the soothing balm that follows your disillusionment about divine inspiration. You don't have to start from scratch. You get to stand on the shoulders of all the other writers, thinkers, composers, choreographers, musicians, painters, sculptors, actors and dancers that came before you. You get to learn from them. You get to take the pickaxe of your imagination into the diamond mines of their ideas and art and chip away. You get to use those bits of sparkle as starting points.

This is an appropriate time for me to stop and say a few words about plagiarism.

A FEW WORDS ABOUT PLAGIARISM

I think we are all already in agreement that we should never, never do it. But it is sometimes difficult to know what it is. Especially in the early years of anyone's writing, when there is great concern with finding, honing, and only using one's "own voice." This is a journey that, by necessity, has no map. We are supposed to discover this thing, our voice, through a long awkward process of sloppy imitation of the writing we admire. But we are not supposed to *imitate* imitate.

Besides directly ripping off someone else's phrases, even paraphrasing without acknowledgement or proper citation is plagiarism. We may be accused of plagiarizing, whether or not we are technically culpable, if our work too closely resembles the voice or imagery of another writer. And often, we don't know we're doing it. We read a poem at some point, and some imagery or line floats around in our heads ever after. We genuinely have no idea where it comes from when it percolates down and lands on the page of a piece we are working on. We are constantly being influenced, if not brain-washed intentionally, by others, in our reading and in our writing and in our lives. (There is a good kind of brain-washing, too. I swear. Look at what JFK and Martin Luther King, Jr. did. I know that's usually called *charismatic persuasion*, but whatever. I've seen and heard footage of them speaking, and both their voices had very hypnotic qualities.)

So let's just all agree that, 1) we should try to hold ourselves to the highest possible standard in this regard, while accounting for the possibility of innocent imitation, and 2) that we would be NOWHERE as artists if we didn't steal each other's ideas. Agreed? Great. Let's move on.

BEGINNINGS

This is a chapter about beginnings. About how to get started writing. It might also be a chapter about the Big Bang of cosmology theory. Or about the zero card in the tarot deck – the Fool.

I was given my first tarot deck as a gift from my older sister when I was thirteen. For the uninitiated in the history and the what of the Tarot, I will try to make this background brief and fascinating. (And if you are not curious, at all, about Tarot or systems of symbology, what are you doing reading a book about writing poetry?) According to James Wanless, the word "tarot" is "an anagram of tota, meaning 'total,' and rota, meaning 'the revolving wheel.'"[5] There are typically 78 cards in a deck, 22 of which are categorized as Major Arcana cards. These are the ones with the big heavy names like "The Priestess" and "Death." The other 56 cards are Minor Arcana and are divided into four categories, often named Swords, Cups, Pentacles, and Wands, but not always. These categories represent, generally and in order, the spheres of the mental, the emotional, the physical, and the act, spirit, or will.

The deck of cards called Tarot is believed to have emerged sometime after the dark ages, as early or as late as the 15th century, and was used in various regions of Europe to play rad card games with. It wasn't until the 18th century that it became what we think of it as today – a system of symbols used by mystics for divination. I don't want to take the time to define divination, or defend my belief in the universality of symbols and archetypes, or explain my passion for systems of self-governance. I want to get to the point, I swear.

The Fool card is the first card in the deck, the zero card. It is often depicted as a child about to walk over the edge of a cliff. If I were a Hollywood party tarot psychic and you drew that card, I might take your money in exchange for telling you that you are about to take a very big, very important risk in your life, and you should do it, and have trust and have faith in the order of the universe. If I were famous occultist Aleister Crowley, I would tell you that the Fool card represents the empty quantum void before the Big Bang. If I were graphic novel overlord Alan Moore, I would tell you, "It's Magic's foremost trick, I guess, how something comes from nothingness."[6] If I were Mindy Nettifee, and we were hanging out and drinking tea and you had a sudden impulse to shuffle my deck and drew The Fool, I would gasp and say, "Oh— you've just drawn the most powerful card."

How we get from *tabula rasa* to the first line of a poem is a moment and act of great electricity, and possibly the most mysterious part of our craft. Even as I move forward to demystifying that moment by passing on tricks of the trade I have learned or absorbed over the years, I want to be grounded in my fascination with this mystery: the relationship between the unconscious mind and conscious thought. The power of that connection and tapping into it.

I am also going to take a leap, like the Fool I am, and suggest that there is a relationship between the unconscious mind and the collective mind, whatever the hell that means. It might have something to do with what I refer to often as "the psychic railroad tracks," and what happens when we feel the rumbling. It might have something to do with our brains and bodies, which are constantly receiving an incomprehensible volume and flow of information, organizing it, changing it, and limiting how much of it we are aware of for the sake of our actual functioning. It might also have something to do with DNA, the double-helixed miracle of how coded information is passed from body to body at conception, the literal source of all of us, the stuff that connects us to our ancestors, and our ancestors' ancestors, and to star dust.

What I have to say about all of this definitively is this: I think it is truly beautiful when humans, small specks that we are, attempt to and believe we can understand the whole. I think writing poetry and using metaphor to try to understand or explain the things we cannot talk about directly, or have no words for, is beautiful. I think great writing that seeks to mean many things at once, to be both microcosm and macrocosm, to play with the connective tissue between all things in order to divine wisdom, is beautiful.

For that beauty, for its constant death and rebirth through art—a moment of silence might be in order. Am I right, John Cage? No? No response? Nothing?

ASSIGNMENT

Let's call this *The Autodidact's Guide To Cultivating Inspiration.* Or *Curiosity Will Not Kill You, Because You Are Not A Cat And That Is Just An Idiom Anyway.* All those other thinkers and artists I told you to stand on the shoulders of? Their work will not just find you. You need to seek it out. And you need their work like you need oxygen. You also need regular doses of non-artistic input from the world around you. Your assignment is to start actively cultivating inspiration and statifying your curiosity. Here are a few suggestions to get you started in this direction:

1. Start in your own backyard.

Be a tourist in your own town! Visit its museums regularly. Hike its trails. Learn its history. Learn about its local flora and fauna. Find someone in their 70s or 80s who has lived there most, if not all, of their lives and interview them. And conversely, *don't be a tourist in your own town.* Consider volunteering at your local community garden or shelter, or becoming a member of a local club of enthusiasts.

2. Get into the news that is not The News.

Have whatever opinion you want on the state of the fourth estate. It is healthy to want to stay current with local and national and international events of historical importance, and some sources are better than others. And it is classic hipster artist to be a total Luddite. But for cultivating inspiration, I suggest you start seeking out non-traditional sources for news. The technological revolution has made this easier than ever. There are stunning science blogs out there from sources as disparate as WIRED magazine and NASA. You can dig in to The Atlantic Monthly's meaty reporting and essaying online. I am also partial to design news sites, where I can see what some genius in Spain has recently done with legos, or hear that someone has invented a new material that will save us all. Bonus tip: there is an entire section of the main library where I live that has complete catalogs of magazines on every subject! I could go right now and nerd out about, well, anything. Have you ever been to your library's periodicals section? Hmmm?

3. Discover music.

If you don't know about Pandora and the music genome project, you do now. Also, the public radio station KCRW has a podcast called "Today's Top Tune" curated by the producers of their music show, Morning Becomes Eclectic. And have you *seen* iTunes's radio show list? New music will stimulate new feelings and ideas in you, and is great for your brain (and sometimes, your dance moves).

4. Develop new obsessions.

Decide right now you are going to fill some holes in your knowledge base, to jump start your own renaissance. I take on new obsessions every couple of months. At different times over the years, I have decided for some reason it was *really* important for me to study fractal geometry, the history of Islam, successful revolutions, the Aztecs, or how to poach an egg perfectly.

CHAPTER 3: THE SOURCE

In my opinion (we can discuss why I feel I have to start this particular sentence with that trope at the end of this book), you should be writing about *you*, about your life, directly from your own source material, the stuff no one else has access to. What makes me love a poem is not only that it has gorgeous language or daring implications or the punch of wisdom; it's that I feel like I have learned something about the writer. I fall in love when I feel no one else could have written what I'm reading.

I am not saying that all your writing should contain an element of direct confession or narrative. Why would I say that? That's like saying, "don't use your imagination to its fullest," or "Meryl Streep can't act." Nor am I ruling out persona poems. Great persona poems arise out of the author's source material, their perspective, their limitless empathy. Cue Patricia Smith's *Skinhead*, or *34*. And I am also not ruling out writing political poetry, or poetic journalism, if you will. Crushingly good writing can come from a poet's individual approach to an idea or theme from history or the body politic. Cue Stephen Dobyn's *White Pig*.

But warning bells go off in me when I read or hear a poem that seems completely ungrounded in the author's real life experiences or perspectives. It's a feeling of ickiness, akin to what I feel when I see someone co-opting another culture's belief systems without any self-awareness about it at all. (See: white shamanism.) If you are going to write about something completely outside of your own experience, something that does not in any way belong to you—say, a war you never fought in and have no personal connection to, or the small, daily traumatic operas of poverty while you are living off a trust-fund—if you are not even going to *try* to connect yourself to it in the writing, to explore textually or subtextually why you are writing about this distant thing, be prepared for something: cognitive dissonance in the reader. Or worse. A direct feeling of emotional manipulation, followed by a rejection of your writing and its premises.

Over the course of your entire life's work, you should try on many personae and voices. You will also explore stories from history and other people's lives that capture your heart and imagination. You should write about whatever you want to write about. I am suggesting you do not *need* to borrow someone else's stories to write great poetry. You already have all the source material you need, whether you know it or not, and that's where your best work will come from.

Your life is unique. The things that have happened to you have not happened to anyone else in exactly the same way. And even if they have, you have remembered and would describe those experiences differently because your perception of what happened got refracted through all your previous stories and experiences. People are cumulative. You are cumulative. Your mind has a shape to it, quite literally, because of all the neuropathways you have built in it. Your specific fears, your specific desires, your specific political kinks—those are yours alone, too. The key word here is *specific*.

Often beginning writers use sweeping, general metaphors. They think the more general they are when they write about something, the more relatable it will be. The opposite is true. It is specific details, not generalities, that make poems resonate. If you are writing from your own source material, you already have the specifics at your disposal. If you are exploring an outside source, you have some serious research to do.

Allow me to illustrate with a short poem of mine from *Sleepyhead Assassins*:

7 THINGS I NEVER TOLD MY OLDER SISTER,
BECAUSE I KNOW BETTER,
IN REVERSE CHRONOLOGICAL ORDER

1. If you ever feel like leaving him, renting a rich blue convertible and becoming someone else somewhere in the desert, I'll go with you.
2. Thank you for all the horrible and/or dangerous things you did first, so I could learn from your mistakes. Specifically: getting herpes, dropping out of school, getting a trendy dream catcher tattoo.
3. I dropped acid with your ex-girlfriend.
4. Remember back during your chunky crystals and channeling spirits phase, when you told me in the back seat of a Ford Taurus that you had spoken with my higher self and she was "really worried about me"? I haven't trusted myself since.
5. I took French in school because you did, and I thought we would be able to have top secret conversations about sex and drugs and rated R films in front of mom. Why didn't we do that?
6. I was the one that destroyed your Black Crowes tape, not the dog.
7. Every time you ran away from home, I followed you.

When I read this poem aloud, it grips the audience with emotional recognition. And it's not because their older sister also got herpes, and also dropped out of high school, and also got a dream-catcher tattoo. It's not because they, too, once dropped acid with their sister's ex-girlfriend, or lied about the destruction of a Black Crowe's tape. It's because when you ground your writing in the specific details of what actually happened, the true stuff of life you could not make up if you tried, you give your work the ring of truth.

And I mean ring like vibration. Like the way sound and light travel. Like the way our bodies receive information. By the time I get to my last line— "Every time you ran away from home, I followed you"—I have transmitted something emotionally universal about the complicated love that sisters, and maybe siblings in general, have for each other. I accomplished this not by saying, "the love of sisters is complex as a rainforest." I accomplished this with concrete, specific details—and maybe when it comes to herpes, *too specific*— about my relationship with my sister. Bless her that she was, and continues to be, incredibly good-natured about my total violation of her privacy for the sake of a poem, and that she still speaks to me.

If you are not already in the habit of this, began keeping a list of things you want to write about someday, when you are ready, or when you have the time. Do not trust that you will remember it. The brain's method of memory storage is a many-chambered, disconnectedly-connected thing. Write the idea down the moment you think of it. It can be a line of conversation you overheard. An image. A story from your past you just remembered and haven't thought about in years. Carry a notebook with you everywhere. Sleep with one. Use your cell phone to call and leave yourself a message. Grab a pen from the waitress' hand like a lunatic, and put it down on a napkin, or your arm. Start a serious collection of these bits of source material, these beginning thoughts. You'll need them.

And if you're having trouble imagining what in the world could or should possibly make it onto this list, go back and re-read the introduction to this book. Anything can go on the list. But the signal that something should definitely go on the list is that it has an emotional charge for you. Remembering it, or realizing you forgot it in the first place for so long, gave you a jolt. If you are terrified of writing about it, if you're afraid of what it means that you feel this way, of what other people would think of you if you wrote about it, if you feel your ego resisting it with every nasty tool in its arsenal—put it on the list. Resolve to go there. I can already feel its pulse.

ASSIGNMENT

Why wait? Start your list right here:

1. Oswaldo
2. Danny
3. dad
4. my fear of being dumb
5. envy + not-envy
6. AA
7. sisters - black sheep - distance. reunion. kindness. The limits of it - role models
8. getting old
9. sleeping w/ a married man
10. harassing sources w/ emails
11. crafting a stupid pitch + getting a tiny ep. boost + feeling terrified That people suddenly hated me b/c I was always the failure + reading dad magazines + feeling disgusted w/ my profession but wanting Everyone to know Politico liked my idea even if I was convinced I would fuck it up + had already

pissed them off w/in like 2
days, or convinced myself
at least that they were pissed.
why?

12. AA beach mtg + the guy who
aggressively asked me if I went
to an AA mtg in the circle,
doubting my ~~sincerity~~ sincerity or
right to be there

13. christian science

14. vampires

15. my father's sister + her family —
    Malynne's visit

16. my mother's sister

17. A single photograph of my
    mother + her mother

18. my grandmother, the myth
    clarissa

19. my mother's canned stories —
    even at glance

ON WRITING POETRY

"There can be no doctor/patient dynamic game going on…
We are all in it together. Shared ignorance. Shared hopes. Shared risks."
—Timothy Leary

"Either you repeat the same conventional doctrines everybody is saying,
or else you say something true, and it will sound like it's from Neptune."
—Noam Chomsky

CHAPTER 4: PRACTICAL MAGIC

First of all, I don't want to hear anything from you if you did not love that movie, and are irritated I just borrowed its name for the title of this section of the book. I stand by my love of it, its title, and all well-crafted "chick flicks." *Back off.*

So! You have all this rich, dense, unique source material to work with. Now what? Here are some literal, practical jumping off points for writing/ prompting poems. Let's call them Poem Cliffs.

Poem Cliffs

—a concrete object
—an idea/thought/philosophy you have and want to express
—something that happened to you
—something that happened to someone else
—a thing someone once said
—an article or Op-Ed in a newspaper or magazine
—a line of someone else's that inspired you
—your broken heart[7]
—your vulnerabilities
—your relationship(s) to:
        your body
        your family
        the places you have lived or live or visited and had vivid experiences
        in
        important people in your life
        people you've excommunicated from your life
        people you've lost; possessions you've lost
        your ego
        your ambition
        your beliefs
        God/Not-God/The Universe
        Nothingness (You tell me the true difference between the
        philosophies of Krishnamurti and Jean-Paul Sartre, and your next
        bourbon or beer or latte or hot chocolate is on me!)
—a structure you want to play with
—a feeling you felt when that song came on the radio
—what's missing in your life
—what's missing in the world

I could go on and on and on. Anything and everything is a beginning. There is no topic too dull and lifeless on the surface that it cannot be worked into a poem. Once you have the initial thought or thread in mind you want to work with, take a deep breath, and center yourself. Depending on what poem-cliff you want to jump off of, the "what comes next" will be different. (It's like a choose-your-own-adventure! I love those!)

The "what comes next" of this book is a series of chapters that explore some of these poem cliffs and how to jump off of them. Because I am fundamentally uncomfortable with the doctor-patient dynamic when teaching or discussing the great creative infinity that is poetry, I decided I could not approach this from an attitude of prescription. Instead, I put *myself* through these exercises, and write poems from them. I then painstakingly try to illuminate my process for you. And then I sum up what I think are the most salient, manifesto-y points to be taken from the exercise.

This approach may not be the right thing for me to do, personally or professionally. I may just be substituting the doctor-patient dynamic for the also-uncomfortable and possibly very unwise patient-patient dynamic. I might be about to wounded-healer bleed all over you, which would be embarrassing for all of us. Or worse: this may be like the magician revealing his secrets. Taboo. But I have a not-so-secret thing against secrets. So. Onward to the cliffs.

CHAPTER 5:
Any Thing Can Be an Instrument

POEM CLIFF: A CONCRETE OBJECT

If you have chosen a concrete object (or been assigned one in a workshop with poet Brendan Constantine, where he just unloaded a box of bizarre treasure onto the classroom floor), the place to begin is by searching yourself for your first-instinct associations with that object.

You can do this internally, or by literally scratching out notes or a mind map on a piece of paper. You can also begin by doing a Writing-Down-The-Bones-style free write. (Shout out to Natalie Goldberg! *Writing Down The Bones* is a classic of the how-to writing genre. Her book should be required reading. In fact, if you haven't read it, I'm officially requiring you to read it.) I think one of Ms. Goldberg's most powerful ideas in that book is also perhaps her simplest: that the basic unit of writing is the timed exercise. Her six rules for the timed writing exercise are: keep your hand moving; don't cross out; don't worry about spelling, punctuation, grammar; lose control; don't think, don't get logical; and go for the jugular.[8]

She explains in more detail, but seriously, if you haven't read it yet, go get it. It is an incredible Zen guidebook for all genres of writing. And her entire point about doing timed free-write exercises is about burning through to what she calls First Thoughts, because your first thought or association or instinct about something often has the most juice or truth in it. Malcolm Gladwell's entire book, *Blink*, is essentially a collection of evidence to support this hypothesis.

My process does not involve this style of free-write very often anymore, though I still return to it every once in awhile, even if just to keep my right-writing-hand-muscles pumped. These days, my process for this sort of direct prompt is more, well…rather than just spending a mad flock of paragraphs trying to describe it, I am going to show you.

I was recently harassed lovingly into returning for an episode of The Lightbulb Mouth Radio Hour. It's a live variety show that has shifted format over the years, but for this particular run they had been experimenting with starting each show with a "found object poetry contest." Competing poets are selected beforehand and sent a photo of an object that was probably purchased, or it's photo snapped, at a Dollar Store or thrift store.

I was sent a photo of a package of fake moustaches. My first thought was, "Oh Christ. I have to write a poem about moustaches?" I sat down, took a breath. I thought about fake moustaches and what they might mean to me. My first thought was of a Halloween costume I chose and my mother cobbled together for me when I was ten-years-old. I had decided I wanted to go trick-or-treating dressed up as a businessman. I have drawn a visual representation of the thought process that occurred in my mind before and during the writing of the piece. (See figure A.)

— FIGURE A.

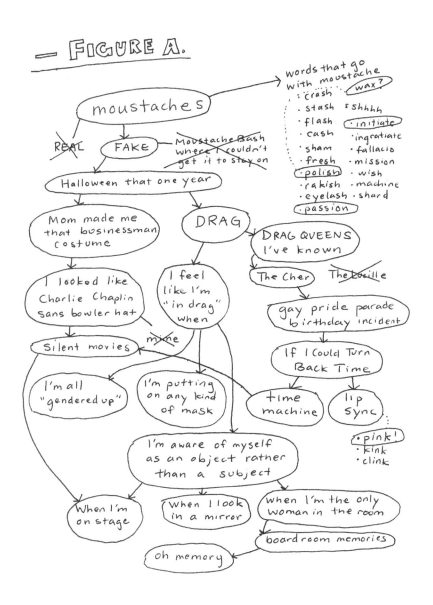

words that go with moustache:
- crash
- stash
- flash
- cash
- sham
- fresh
- polish
- rakish
- eyelash
- passion
- wax?
- shhhh
- initiate
- ingratiate
- fallacio
- mission
- wish
- machine
- shard
- pink!
- kink
- clink

moustaches

REAL   FAKE   Moustache Bash where I couldn't get it to stay on

Halloween that one year

Mom made me that businessman costume

DRAG

DRAG QUEENS I've known

The Cher   The Lucille

I looked like Charlie Chaplin sans bowler hat

I feel like I'm "in drag" when

gay pride parade birthday incident

Silent movies   mine

If I Could Turn Back Time

I'm all "gendered up"

I'm putting on any kind of mask

time machine   lip sync

I'm aware of myself as an object rather than a subject

When I'm on stage   When I look in a mirror   when I'm the only woman in the room

boardroom memories

oh memory

Here is the piece of poetry that came out of a photo of fake moustaches:

THE YELLOW BRICK ROAD

The only time I dressed in drag was my tenth Halloween
when I wanted to go as a "businessman"
which was the scariest thing I could think of.

My mother indulged me, got me a fake moustache, a suit,
tailored it. We hid my long blond hair in a discreet bun.
Most people thought I was a poorly executed Charlie Chaplin.

I haven't dressed in drag since, because, well,
soon after, I estrogened like Spring pollens.
I swole up, I blossomed, I was initiated into the long,

wet, red-walled path into becoming a woman.
It was much more complicated than trying to look like a man.
Female or male, putting on heels and make up and a dress is drag.

Learning to smile a certain way to disarm without appearing
vulnerable is drag. Learning to see how you are seen,
then managing your own objecthood with the ornaments

of clothing, posture, tone of voice, vocabulary–drag.
My thirteenth birthday landed on the same day
as the Long Beach Pride Parade, and my father lived in a porched

apartment on Broadway, so I got to watch the whole show while
sipping sodas from the fridge. At some point, the floats stalled.
The tallest most outrageous Cher I'd ever seen descended

from her platform, parted the sidewalk crowd to reach me,
grabbed my hand and lipsticked it, then said, "Sweetie,
you're so pretty, you make me want to turn the page."

I swooned. I had been anointed by a High Priestess
of everyone-can-go-to-hell-don't-I-look-fabulous.
She winked at me, and it slow-mo-ed extra with her long false lashes.

She lady-swaggered back, pulling applause behind her like
so many pink satin trains, and then launched into an impassioned
lip sync of If I Could Turn Back Time. If I could turn back time,

I wouldn't change anything. But I would watch it all again,
an audience to the silent movie of my life.
I'd gasp when I saw myself get on a stage for the first time.

I'd laugh tenderly at myself looking at myself in the mirror,
puzzled, embarrassed, uncertain, pretending grace. I'd cry
tears of catharsis when I saw myself suited and seated in that

board room of men, learning the hard way how to make a poker face.
How to hide my feelings, my truth, deep inside me like an emerald
in my gut, where I could polish and polish and polish.

★ ★ ★

Now that you've studied the hand-drawn Mindy's-mind-map and read the
poem, I want to highlight several things that may not be immediately obvious.
The map is my attempt to show you visually what my flow of thoughts looks
like. It's a little scattered, very free-associate-y, but there is order to it, too.
There are ideas I have and reject, and ideas I choose to move forward with. I
make these choices based on which ideas have the most charge or electricity
for me at the moment. And yes, they are often my "First Thoughts." But not
always.

My default style of writing at this point in my development is what I'm
randomly deciding to call, right this second, "mixed-narrative-philosophical."
I am both trying to tell stories from my life and trying to express ideas I have,
ideas I may not even know I have until I am writing them, until I am at the
moment of articulation. So naturally for me, in this instance, I started with
telling the story of the only time I've ever dressed in drag. I chose this story
in part because, well, there was really only the one time I ever dressed in drag
and successfully wore a fake moustache, and that was it. Also, I hadn't thought
about that Halloween since that Halloween, and the sudden vivid memory
of trick-or-treating in a shoddy homemade costume through the "rich
neighborhoods," where my costume intention was not obvious because of its
low-production value, had a lot of unexpected emotional charge for me.

This is what I mean about being brave. I chose to start with that story because
it scared me what would come out. It is terrifying for me still, to write about
the stuff of my childhood, when we were poor and I was just starting to
realize it, when my mom was hard-working and superhuman but also prone,
of course, to nervous breakdowns at Christmas-o-clock, when my father
was living openly as a gay man, and got the standard sparse divorced-father

visitation rights, and he was in many ways a vulnerable, fragile stranger to me, who I had a great power to hurt and vice-versa. It's also terrifying for me to write about any of my experiences being raised in the gay community, before and after I knew what sex was, because it's really precious and important to me, how that shaped me. At the time of the Pride Parade described in the poem, George H.W. Bush was president, following 8 years of Ronald Reagan, and AIDS was rampant. A lot of good people who deserved full blazing lives were rotting in hospice beds and dying horrific deaths. The conservatives in power were indifferent, or openly hostile, and certainly willfully ignorant. I'm saying not only is it hard for me to go there, I also just don't want to fuck it up.

And good lord—redefining "drag" from the bias of a mostly-straight female-identified female? RISKY. But I knew there was something there, so I kept going. And then I had the Cher memory—oh, how could I not have written about that before? Talk about delicious source material. So I switched gears and started telling that story, without over thinking it or inventing connective tissue or forcing flow. This employs a tactic I often use, and picked up from reading the essays of Kurt Vonnegut collected in the delightful book *Wampeters, Foma, and Granfalloons.* (Another book I strongly recommend.) In his essays, he radically veers off course constantly, without warning, and then ties it all up at the end. I worship his essay style. As might be growing obvious to you by now.

So then, there I was. I had started from the object inspiration of the fake moustache, told two stories, and connected them loosely with some thoughts I had about a larger definition of the meaning of the word "drag." I had stopped at the song title *If I Could Turn Back Time*, and just for kicks, I really wanted my next line to be, "If I could turn back time." (Rule # 2,642: if you are not having any fun at all, knock it off.) I had to figure out how to Vonnegut this thing. How to tie it up. When you reach this point in your poem writing, I strongly suggest you revisit the beginning of your poem. I am obsessed with symmetry, or intentional asymmetry, in poems. I like it when the end of a poem has an echo or ring of the beginning in it, even if it is a shadow echo or opposite ring. (This is just a frequent personal preference for my own writing. I do deviate from it, so in no way is this a process rule. There are amazing poets out there who personally prefer to drop you off a cliff at the end of the poem, every time, ending abrupt as a heart attack. It's a stylistic choice. One of several million available to you. Done well, it has the impact of a cut. It stings with meaning, with unresolved emotion. It leaves you pregnant with questions and new thoughts.)

In this case, I was interested in the comparison I made of my costume to "a poorly executed Charlie Chaplin," which, though that really happened, seemed random as an image in the poem. So I started wondering about how to suggest Charlie Chaplin in the end, how to get his ghost in there. After playing with a few associations, the ideas of mime and silent movies (as you can see on the map), I went straight for silent movies. That I could find a connection between silent movies and going back in time seemed clear. And then I asked myself the very same question Cher asked herself in the late 80s and wrote a song about– what would I do if I could turn back time? And I simultaneously asked, what in the world does that have to do with silent movies? Well, I won't condescend to over-explain what happened next to you. You read the poem.

I just want to point out two more things – in the top right corner of the map is a thing I am always doing when writing, whether I write it down or it's just streaming through my head. I use my ever-expanding vocabulary to generate and sort through words that have consonance, assonance, alliteration, or internal rhyme with the other word choices I have already made. I seek out consistency in sound. I am going to get WAY more into this in the chapters on editing. But for now I wanted to simply point out that, though this list isn't where the ending of the poem came from, it's one of the reasons I knew I liked it. Polish. Moustache. It has exactly the kind of sound symmetry I go for.

And finally, the title. "Where the hell did that come from?" it is possible you are asking. I believe it is a waste of a title if your title does not add information to the poem; if it does not indicate, directly or indirectly, what your overall meaning is. Use your titles! Use them wisely. Play with them. Stretch them to their title edges. Plant seeds of doubt and epiphany in them for the jury of your readers.

In this case, I wanted to add some information about the meaning of the final stanza, and really the whole piece, with my title. I wanted to answer the question, whether or not it was asked, "Why did she choose an emerald?" Without the title, one might wonder: is the emerald significant because of green imagery somewhere else in the poem I should go re-look at? No! Is it because she is born in May, and that's her birthstone! Yes! But no! Is it because it is common practice to polish rocks inside the body in some culture I've never heard of, and does that have a meaning I am not aware of? No! At least I don't think so. But you don't have to wonder. I told you everything in the title. In this poem, I am on my way to the Emerald City. That means, like, *a lot of things*. I am going out on a steady limb here with this title, and assuming most of my readers will recognize immediately a reference to the

Wizard of Oz. I am assuming they will understand at least a little something about how it is a story of a female's Hero Journey. (You know, like how almost every other myth narrative is about a man's Hero Journey. I'm looking at you, Joseph Campbell.[9])

Finally, I am assuming that this additional concrete indication that I am writing a poem about the path to becoming a woman in this day and age, even though the poem is also clearly about that in everything it says, will add to the reader's resounding, humming, delicious feeling of GETTING IT. That's what most of us want in the end, after all. That's why we're writing. We want someone to understand us, to see us. To *get* us. If we could say what we're trying to say any other way, we wouldn't have to write the poems. And because human psychology is based on projection, that feeling is also what we want to get out of reading other people's poems—that moment of recognition, where we see some part of ourselves reflecting back at us, winking.

SUMMARY:

- Don't forget to breathe and ground yourself. Intentionally. It helps with everything.

- Any object, no matter how absurd or ill-fitting or mundane, can be the opening to writing a poem.

- Get your writing-blood flowing using healthy doses of free-association, whether through a free write, or a brainstorm or mind-map, or by letting your mind wander wherever it wants to. This kind of detached, loose, worm-hole-travel-thinking will help you tap IN.

- Make your content choices based on the emotional charge or electricity they have for you, personally.

- Take risks.

- Drift. Allow yourself to write without over thinking, over-logic-ing, and over-connecting things. You will have time later to edit and tighten and tie up anything that needs tying up.

- Use your beginnings to create your endings. Use your endings to recreate your beginnings.

- Pay attention to the musicality of your word choice, to consistency and rhythm of sound. Use all the poetic devices at your disposal to make your poem sing.

- Use your titles. They are one of your most powerful tools for forging meaning.

- Be intentional about your meaning. Even when you don't exactly know what you mean.

ASSIGNMENT

You've just discovered an old wooden box someone left out by the trash. It has a metal lock on it that's been bent, like someone recently broke into it, and it clinks as you pick it up. You take it back to your living room, open it, and dump the contents on the floor. Here is what you find:

- an antique pocket watch

- an elevator button

- a letter opener

- a restaurant matchbook with a phone number written on it

- a magnifying glass

- a Gordian knot

- a snow globe with a miniature city in it

- one earring

- a small statue of the Hindu deity Ganesh

- a mineral rock of some sort you cannot identify

- an old dictionary with the entire "R" section ripped out

- an old cassette tape labeled "To Jackie"

Pick one of the objects up, and using everything you gleaned from this chapter, turn it into a poem.

CHAPTER 6:
THE METAPHYSICS OF STORYTELLING

POEM CLIFF: SOMETHING THAT HAPPENED TO YOU

This one should be the easiest one for me. Narrative poetry is where I live. But I will tell you right now, there is nothing easy about this for me. Nor, I imagine, for you.

Our stories, the things "that happened to us," are both our blessing and our curse as writers. The blessing part should be obvious. If electric, horrifying, edifying, fascinating, out-of-the-ordinary, oh-hell-no-that-did-not-just-happen things have happened to you, your source-cup is over-flowing. You will never *not* have things to write about. Whether you want to write about those things is another story entirely. (It might be the story you're reading at this moment. Shhhh!) But we're pretending to be brave and impervious to our misgivings and fears and not-my-comfort-levels, remember?

The curse part. Let's discuss.

We live in a world of opposites. Black and white. Right and wrong. Male and female. North and south. In the biz, (the biz of divining wisdom, of wisdoming,) we know that the idiom "the other side of the coin" is not just there for Irony to play with. We know that everything indicates or contains its opposite, its shadow. Enlightenment junkies everywhere know that Truth is found in the in-between, or the unification, or what I think I heard a Hindu woman describe to me as "the Nagwal."

So here is the curse that has to come with the blessing, the dark shadow of writing and story-telling: being too attached to the narratives of your life, the stories of "what happened to you," can also make you crazy. Wait, I should have spelled that Crazy. It can keep you from being able to experience being in the present moment with awakeness and clarity; from knowing that everything that is happening right now is *brand new*. It has not happened before. Attachment to "your story" can keep you locked in an unhealthy relationship with the voice(s) in your head, or your ego, the thing that is an Expert on everything, because it has already been there and done that and come back with knowledge about how Everything Is. It can block you from learning new things, or experiencing what is actually happening without the filter of all your baggage. Most importantly, it can just cause you a lot of suffering. You can be emotionally and mentally locked in a place where you live in your past, and it defines everything for you. That past might be a very dark place. And though you are right to search, and remember, and feel, and grieve; you need to know that whenever you need some relief, it is available to you. Right NOW.[10]

I meant it when I said "you are cumulative." You are everything that has ever happened to you, and all the you's you have ever been, at 2, 6, 13, 22, etcetera. But *you* are also not the voice in your head, the narrator. The stream-of-consciousness thinker that thinks, "oh, here we go again. This always happens to me. Nothing will ever change." *You* are the part of you that is aware of that voice that hears it. You can remember that whenever you want, and let the voices peter out, let the stories of your past pain that are creating real suffering for you in the present go quiet.

And who is the You that is aware of the *you*? I don't know. Ask Dr. Seuss. He seems to know that type of stuff.

So you need your stories, your source material, to write from. And you also may need to completely detach from your stories most of the time to cope and live in the moment and feel joy. And also the process of writing about your stories may be the very trick to freeing yourself from their power over you. And also you need to wrestle with their power, and give them more of it, so that the writing will be Frankensteinian, and given frightening, exhilarating life. I've said what I needed to say about this. We may as well all get used to eating paradox for breakfast. On to the exercising. (Exorcising?)

A story I have long wanted to write about has to do with the Wizard of Oz. (Are you wondering now if every exercise I write in this book will have something to do with the Wizard of Oz, or girl-woman stuff, or iconic Gay culture stuff? Wouldn't that be great if it was true? Are we having a big old glittery poetry party or what?) I wanted to tell the story of how I watched the movie many times in black and white before I saw it in color or, rather, Technicolor. And that the first time I saw it in color, the first time I saw the Munchkin Land in full rainbow gaga, my brain changed. Completely. I was a kid. It was some sort of natural LSD thing.

Until now, though, I've started it a dozen times at least and never finished even a draft. I nearly always struggle with how to start narrative poems. Not just because the stories are important to me (see previous chapter), but for practical reasons. Sometimes I just can't get a handle on a point of entry. I want to avoid using common openers like "The first time" or "The only time" or "The last time" or, though I've never used this one, "Once upon a time." But *whatever*—sometimes that's just how the story begins. Even if the poem doesn't end up with that opener ultimately, if it's the phrase you feel you need to just get started, start with it. We're here to tell the story, to pull the trigger on it, not to think on it some more.

Of course, restrictions are always helpful. Restrictions pull us back down to the earth paper when we are in a spiraling, expanding universe of ideas. But, strikes and gutters, dear readers—there are no hard rules to storytelling, in poetry or other forms. If you want restrictions, you are going to have to arbitrarily invent them for yourself each time. Feel free to do that whenever you need to—arbitrarily invent some rules for your poem.

Otherwise, it's a free-for-all. You do not need to start at the beginning. You can and should experiment with chronology whenever you feel like it. You can start in the middle: in medias res. You can tell the story backwards. (Cue Bob Hicok's amazing "Backward Poem" that starts with the line, "The poem ends in death so I'll walk it/backward home."[11]) You can tell the story completely out of order and find out what happens to it. You can also take a stiff shot of Hemmingway to the head, and tell it plainly and straight-forwardly, in order, with short stabbing sentences.

Another important idea I want to plant in your head about narrative writing—you do not need to tell the whole story. You can show just as much or as little of it as you think is necessary for the poem to work, for your meaning to get across. The incomparable poet and teacher Rachel McKibbens puts it something like this, and I am paraphrasing: a poem is a window into a room. The reader is on the outside, looking in. That window has curtains. You, the writer, control the curtains. You control how much or how little you reveal, how much light or shadow you want to shed.[12] Rachel is also often instructing her students to not tell the story at all; just describe the aftermath. She has a PhD in Aftermath Math. Check out *Pink Elephant* if you don't believe me.

Lastly, before the stories start boiling inside of us, and we are all staring at blank pages and panicking about the work of it and how to start, let's remember the great thing about writing poems—it's about play. Word play. And words can have a lot of different meanings, depending on their context, where and how you choose to place them, what words they are next to, what words they aren't, and what words are missing. Words can mean many things at once. Your poem can mean many things at once. The story you are telling can be one story AND it can be one hundred stories. At the *same time*. You are a Jungian sorcerer, playing with the symbols your words and images create, twisting myths from them. You are a weaver; the poem is your cloth. Invent a new pattern with it. Reference other patterns in your new pattern. Unweave it when you don't like it. Reweave it differently. Repeat. Don't be afraid to write and rewrite this baby as many times as you need to. As my 6th grade home economics teacher once sang out like a Victorian Mother Goose, "As ye sew so shall ye rip."

This time, I am not going to draw you a ridiculous Mindy-mind-map. I am instead going to show you the actual first draft of the poem. I still mostly write by hand, with a pen or pencil and paper, old school. I started writing pre-computer. There is a hard-wired line from my imagination to my right hand. And not only do I find it jarring to my process to be at a keyboard, staring at the glow of a blank Word document screen, but computers don't let me do the messy thing I do when I'm writing, the thing I'm about to show you. I am often writing something relatively fast, trying to get the idea out while it's hot, and so I do not bother with erasing or any of that nonsense. I just get my marginalia on, and my cross outs, and my carets. Sometimes it ends up looking like a psychotic (if highly-fine-motor-skilled) howler monkey wrote it. Sometimes it looks like a tree with arrows for leaves. Sometimes it looks a whole lot like the mind-map, just without the mappy neatness. And for the record, to any of you amateur or professional handwriting analysts out there, I *know*, okay?

MY ENTIRE AESTHETIC CAN BE TRACED BACK TO THIS MOMENT

by the time my father got a color television
with a VHS player, I had already seen
The Wizard of Oz at least twenty times
in black and white.
I could not understand his sparkling glee
as he made the popcorn,   brightened eyes.
the salesman's closing pitch in his ~~smile~~
                                                Lord I loved
                                                this movie

the movie started like it always did —
with Kansas and the farm and the song
and Judy's curls   and the voice Her fierce   with the evil
lady, I knew ~~would~~ be the wicked witch . With
Toto, and Auntie Em's fierce midwest
hate face and the nasty Dunaway, and   fortune teller
the ~~~~ shady turbaned ~~~~ Clark Kent,
~~to the all~~ powerful Wizard, and the
tornado, and the house flying up
in to it.
and then the house lands ~~and~~ it's so quiet.   Dorothy tip toes
my father is bursting at his father seams.   carefully.
~~and~~ ~~Dorothy~~ she opens the door.   Bewildered.
                                                   curious.

spinning spinning song.

FIGURE B

Here is the poem that came out of that, in a form you can actually read:

MY ENTIRE AESTHETIC CAN BE TRACED
BACK TO THIS MOMENT

By the time my father got a color television set
and a VHS player I had already seen *The Wizard of Oz*
at least twenty times in black-and-white.

I could not understand the sparkling glee
with which he made the popcorn, the salesman's
closing pitch in his brightened eyes.

The movie started like it always did,
Lord I loved this movie,
with Kansas and the farm and the song

and Judy's curls and that voice. *Her voice!*
With the horrible woman I knew was the Wicked Witch.
With Toto, and Auntie Em's fierce Midwest hate face,

and the hasty runaway, and the shady-turbaned
Clark Kent fortune teller, and the race home,
and the tornado, and the house flying up into it,

and the spinning and spinning and spinning.
Then the house lands. It is so quiet.
Dorothy looks around bewildered.

She tiptoes carefully out of the bedroom. Curious.
My father is bursting at his father seams.
She opens the door.

★ ★ ★

You would have bet for the narrative poetry chapter I would have gone BIG,
right? Hit you with a heart-breaking poem-hammer forged from prison
wardens' nightmares and the wishing-star-children of Yeti-dreams? Well,
that didn't happen. You never know what's going to happen when you sit
down to write a poem. This is the poem that came out. I thought, too, that

I was giving myself the chance to go balls-out on some hallucinogenic Oz descriptions. But the moment I wrote the word "door," I knew it was done.

One of the things I hated about being taught poetry in school was that there was a total, tunnel-visioned emphasis on just getting us to identify devices. I'm sure this had something to do with test preparation, but it was infuriating. "Can you point out a metaphor in this poem? A simile? Can you identify instances of consonance and assonance?" There was never a discussion of what any of it meant. So let's change the post-poem break down for this exercise. Let's dig in to the whys. To do this proper, I am going to adopt a sort of pseudo-self-Socratic-method-mode. Ahem:

What is this narrative poem about? Is it about the first time I got to see The Wizard of Oz in color? Yes. Is it about how much I love that movie, and Judy Garland, and how you can fall in love with something's essence before you've even seen it in all its showy glory? Yes. Does that imply anything significant about my philosophy on perception and voyeurism and the inception of meaning? Why, yes it does! Is it about meta-story-telling, since I'm writing a story about a story in a chapter about how to write stories? *Oh my yes.* Does my repetition of the word "spinning," as in *spinning a tale* help indicate this? Yes. Did I discover as I was writing it that The Wizard of Oz might have taught me everything I know about foreshadowing, even though I was too young to grasp that at the time? Yes, that happened. Did that mean I needed to change gears totally, and make the poem itself a foreshadow? Yes, exactly. Is it interesting to me, to think and write about foreshadow or shadow when I'm also writing about the power of color, of Technicolor? Yes!

Is this also a poem about my relationship with my father? Yes, of course. Is it a poem about the parent-child relationship, and the way our parents' shape us, for better or worse, like the Gods they are? Spot on. Is this a story about how I felt for my father, that he had so few opportunities to parent me and my sisters at all, and even less opportunities to do it well because my mom got to see us at least twenty-times as much? Yes. Does my mom have a fierce Midwest hate face too? Oh heck yes. Does that mean this poem is also about her in a way? Uh huh. Was she very protective of us girls? Oh yes. Is that connected at all to the words I chose to describe Professor Marvel, who is also the Wizard, who was a man with great power but who was a bit of a charlatan, a man who hid in plain sight and chose not to be his best most Super Self, and who then in the movie is eventually revealed to be a big faker, full of sound and fury and bluster and showiness, signifying nothing? Which makes him an awful lot like my dad? Yes. Does the fact that in the story being referenced, the all-powerful-wizard turns out to be just a normal man mean anything about my suspicion of all authority figures—fathers, mothers, politicians, preachers, or even entire institutions of power? Wow! Yes.

What am I communicating with my title? That I had an experience at a young age which permanently changed me? Which made me passionate about bright saturated monochrome colors? That made me love everything vivid? Yes. Did that new love of the vivid lead at all to my love of poetry, and the work I do now? Yes. Does it indicate that I am fully embracing the ways in which I *am* my father, I *am* the wizard, the charlatan blusterer who also has some real science magic up his sleeves but knows sometimes you have to put on a show? Yes. That I am also embracing my Dorothyness, that I am a girl from the Midwest, on a path through my art to discover the power I have inside me, the power that was there all along? Yes! That I am also embracing my Auntie-Em-ness, that I am acknowledging my actualization as a mother-figure, or the archetypal Priestess/Protector/Preserver? Yes. (Side note: I am quite literally her now, as I have finally become an aunt, and my name begins with an M, and I insist on being called Auntie M.) Am I shouting out , through the connection of the title to the last line, that I am all about discovery now, about opening doors, about seeing what's on the other side, no matter how unprepared or scared I am? YES.

How did I accomplish all that in twenty lines? How can one story mean so many things at once? Is this seventh-level jujitsu communication? Is this what I'm talking about when I say poetry, and its building blocks of metaphor and imagery and symbolism, are the most powerful tools for transmission of story and knowledge and wisdom? How am I being changed, right now, by coming out from behind my All Powerful Poet curtain, and showing you the levers and smoke machines of how I really do this?

SUMMARY:

- Narrative poetry is not only an incredible way to tell a story. Learning to dance and wrestle with your own stories, to turn them on or off, to change them through the telling of them, to wield or drain their power is potentially VERY nutritious for you emotionally , mentally and spiritually.

- How you get started doesn't matter as much as getting started. You can take all the time you need to work and rework and play and unplay and weave and unweave until you get it to say what you want it to say. Repeating the John Cage chant: begin anywhere.

- Restrictions can be very helpful. Forcing yourself to write in a particular structure, using only words that begin with vowels, limiting your phrases or lines or stanzas to a particular length—it can be very liberating. If you are experiencing too many ideas at once, try it.

- Experiment! With chronology! With syntax! With arrangement! With punctuation! With TYPOgraphy! With everything!

- You do not need to tell the whole story. One piece can be a microcosm of the whole. One moment and its mood can say everything about what created and preceded it.

- Wield your vocabulary. Play with your words. Try different ones on for size, invent new ones when you can't find the right one. Be aware that every word choice you make will be analyzed under the microscope of some total stranger. Hopefully there is some vocab-exhibitionist in you.

- If the story is hot at your fingertips, write fast! Write messy! Seize that sucker! Writing quickly will also help you in your quest to stay in a consistent tone-of-voice, if that indeed matters to the poem-at-hand.

- You never know what poem is going to come out of the writing process. Let go of your expectations while writing it. Amazing, unexpected things will happen.

- When crafting your narrative poem, select guiding metaphors that support, at every level of interpretation, the story you are trying to tell.

- Apply the same approach as a Jungian analyst interpreting dreams. Everything can mean anything, and anything can mean everything. Seek to make your poems work on that Meta level. It's so satisfying.

ASSIGNMENT

"The poet is a liar who always speaks the truth." It was Jean Cocteau who said that. All creative writers with blooming imaginations have a healthy dose of liar in them. Whether you use our powers for the good of truth telling or the evil of ill-intentioned deception is another story, and maybe you should write it. But I digress. Jean does that to me. Here's your assignment:

1. Make a list of three lies you have told.

2. Look at your list. Whichever one you have the most emotional charge around—regret, embarrassment, fear—that's the one you're going to dig into.

3. Do some free-writing for awhile about the lie. Who did you lie to? What were the circumstances? Why did you tell the lie? What were the consequences? Were you ever "found out"? Have you kept this lie a secret? There is a story in here you need to tell.

4. Consider making the title of the piece the lie you told. Then make the poem itself about one or all of the following:
   - The truth
   - The aftermath
   - The why
   - Better lies you could have told
   - What you wish you had done differently

CHAPTER 7: Notes From the Nebula

POEM CLIFF: YOU HEARD OR READ OR SAW SOMETHING THAT SPARKED SOMETHING IN YOU

The first two exercises concentrated on very concrete, definitive writing-cliff-jump-offs. But writing ideas are often from much more nebulous origins. I love that word, "nebulous." It conjures, for me, photos of frozen swirling masses of stars, the swooping anti-gravity feeling I get in my stomach every time I'm in a high-rise elevator, the swoon I experience when I really try to picture the Earth I am standing on spinning and revolving through the Milky Way. Also: everything perfect Carl Sagan ever said.[13]

With our without nebula clouding about, I often think of my mind as a sky. It definitely has weather patterns. Like the weather, its patterns are cyclical and predictable, and also very unexpected things happen—out-of-nowhere cold fronts collide with warm fronts; there are late frosts and Indian summers. Sometimes, while peacefully drinking my morning coffee, feeling like all my parts are in place, I begin to smell a storm coming.

I've encouraged you to seek the inspiration and sustenance of other art as often as possible. But what do you do when you have just read a haunting paragraph, or seen a painting that stained your visual cortex? What do you do when a song comes on the jukebox and interrupts everything and something indefinable blossoms in you, and then rots, and then blossoms, and then rots, and then blossoms?

I am not certain what the difference is, if any, between a feeling and a thought or idea. The excellent program RadioLab, produced out of WNYC by the two science-story-telling geniuses Jad Abumrad and Robert Krulwich, has an episode called Words that I implore you to listen to if you haven't already. I want to share with you some of the most transformative, meta-poetic ideas I extracted from it.[14-begin]

The episode starts with an interview with Susan Schaller, the author of *A Man Without Words*. In that book, and in her interview, she tells of the story of her relationship with a man she calls Ildefonso, a 27-year-old Mayan she met in the late 1970s. Susan became—thanks to a car accident, an ensuing head injury, a recommendation from a friend that she crash classes at the local community college to cure her boredom, the random opening of a door, and the sight of someone drawing pictures in the air with their hands—fluent in sign language, at a time when not many people were. She met Ildefonso in a reading class for the deaf, where she noticed him immediately because he kept himself apart from the others. She introduced herself by signing, "Hello, my name is Susan." Ildefonso signed back, "Hello, my name is Susan." She tried again, and he continued to mime or copy her, rather than reply. She observed him and soon decided that he was not impaired in any way; she defends in her interview, "you can actually see intelligence in the eyes." She had realized: *he has no language.* He didn't know there was *sound.* He would watch everyone talking to each other, moving their mouths and hands, and he thought everyone was communicating to each other visually. Ildefonso assumed he was stupid.

Susan decided she was going to help Ildefonso discover language, and how she did it is incredible, but you can go listen to the podcast of the episode to hear about that. What caught my breath was her description of his moment of epiphany: "He looks as if he had just landed from Mars, and it is the first time he ever saw anything…then he slaps his hands on the table." He *gets it.* "Oh! Everything has a name." He collapsed, and started crying. After her experiences teaching Ildefonso, Susan believes that not only does having words change our thinking, it transforms objects themselves. Once a table is called a "table," it actually *looks* different. Symbolic sound doesn't just initiate shared meaning. It transforms the way we actually see the world.

The next idea from this episode that blew my mind all over my dashboard arrives in the next segment of the show, which alternates between interviewing the scientist Charles Fernyhough, author of *A Thousand Days of Wonder*, and the Harvard University cognitive psychologist who studies babies, Elizabeth Spelke. Through a series of experiments, it has been discovered that until about the age of six, humans do not have the ability to connect discrete elements of information. Do you remember having to learn to say the pledge of allegiance when you were in kindergarten, and how you were supposed to put your right hand over your heart when you did it, and how difficult and clumsy it was to remember which hand was which? Were you taught to turn your hands into L's, and then to look at them, and the one that looked like an L and not a backwards L was your Left hand? This is because your brain had not yet developed the use of spatial language.

The implications of this scientific work are far more radical than just chronologizing brain development landmarks. Elizabeth puts it like this, and I paraphrase: a child's brain is like a series of islands, with "color" on one island, "objects" on another, and "spatial ideas" like left/right/up/down on another. It is the phrase itself—"the cup of milk is to the right of the red apple," for example—that creates the internal connections between the islands, literal neuropathways joining different systems within a single mind. And until about six-years-old, your brain has not developed the ability to build those pathways. But it is *the words themselves*, or rather putting them into phrases and sentences, that does the building. She goes on to summarize, "Language is a fundamentally combinatorial system."

The show then introduce a final twisting question: how do you define thinking? Charles concludes that, "If you reflect on your own experience, much of what's going on in your mind is verbal. I want to suggest [controversially] that the essential thread of all that is actually language, a stream of inner speech." Elizabeth on-the-other-hands, "the stuff I am mostly thinking of when I'm reflecting is the stuff I can't put into words." And then Jad throws in the evidence of music. "A musical phrase is a form of thought," he posits, "a sequence of ideas and emotions…" Elizabeth is then allowed to finish *her* thought, saying, "But there's something we gain access to when we gain a full natural language, that we can use not only to communicate with other people, but with ourselves." Robert, always eager to wrap it up, goes on to say, "[so] you have words now, and you have words in combination now. Now you can play with the combination," and Jad closes out the sentence, in classic RadioLab style, saying, "and that…opens up a kind of inifinity."[14-end]

It is this infinity we are confronted with now, when we are presented with the challenge of articulating a hazy, out-of-focus feeling or thought or idea, or "the stuff" Elizabeth says she is exploring when she is reflecting. We have to perform the trick of putting the what-why-oh-aha fuzz buzz into words. Into the start of a poem. The act of performing this trick might transform the thing itself, whatever it is, from the seed it started as to--what? What do we change when we give something a name?

I am approaching this chapter differently than the last two by putting all my process-revelation and self-analysis upfront, ahead of the poem. (Rule #4,348: switch it up). I am going into the exercise using several "feelings" or "unworded thoughts" I have brewing and building up a storm in me right now. They originate from a song, a poem, and a recent column by Maureen Dowd in the New York Times (NYT). This brings up an important point: there is rarely only one feeling we are trying to pin down and interrogate. And even if it is one feeling, feelings are not static; they move. That's what they want to do. So, on to the three things pulling at my threads today.

A SONG

The song that is haunting me right now (and has been, for years) is a recorded performance of a Mozart composition titled "Fish Beach" on Michael Nyman's album *Revisiting The Don*. I found this album after watching the film *Man On Wire*, a documentary that explores the origins and aftermath of an event on August 7th, 1974, when a young Frenchman named Philippe Petit stepped out on a wire illegally rigged between the New York World Trade Center's twin towers. After dancing for nearly an hour on the wire, he was arrested, taken for psychological evaluation, and brought to jail before he was finally released.[15] The film is stunning—stun-gun stunning. And after seeing it, I became obsessed with its soundtrack, which led me to this album. Anyway. I am listening to the song Fish Beach, on repeat, as I write this next paragraph.

It starts with deep base and baritone sounds, warm welcoming horns. The music makes me feel, at first, a sort of dawning. A powerful sense that something is about to happen. Something BIG. Then the musical phrasing changes, perhaps we are moving into exposition; syncopation begins; an urgency is added. My pulse starts racing. I am moving towards the Something; its arrival is imminent. Then the high strings come in and I am hopeful, joyful, proud maybe. Then the music is retracting, though I am not sure it's a coda. There are hints of mourning, one high longing melody. Is this failure? Am I digging in the earth? Am I burying something, or planting something? No, definitely planting. There is no resolution.

A POEM

I have also just been handed this morning the work of Tomas Tranströmer by a friend, a collection titled *The Finished Heaven* of poems chosen and translated by Robert Bly. Tomas is a famous Swedish writer who I have never heard of before, and who has just been awarded the Nobel Prize in Literature. I am about to find out why. The first poem my friend is eager for me to read is *Guard Duty*.[16] Its last two stanzas go like this:

But to be where I am…and to wait.
I am full of anxiety, obstinate, confused.
Things not yet happened are already here!
I feel that. They're just out there:

a murmuring mass outside the barrier.
They can only slip in one by one.
They want to slip in. Why? They do
one by one. I am the turnstile.

This poem is filled with an incredible silence. Or space. Bly attributes this to the fact that the "four or five main images in each poem come from widely separated sources in the psyche. His poems are a sort of railway station where trains that have come enormous distances stand briefly in the same building."[17] But Tomas has managed to literally describe some of what came up for me in listening to Fish Beach—this feeling that, "Things not yet happened are already here!" That Something is coming, or has come and has not come. But that it wants to. And it is requiring something of me, some work, some planting of a seed so that it might bloom into existence through me. *I am the turnstile.* Neuropathways are drawing themselves in my brain.

A COLUMN

The final thing that's been nagging at me is one of Maureen Dowd's notorious op-eds for the New York Times. This one is titled "Don't Tread On Us." It is a response to the latest outbreak of what she calls "mass misogyny" in America or, more specifically, in the leadership of the Republican Party. Her column deftly weaves together commentary on Secretary of State Hillary Clinton's political past, present and future, the Republican's "chilling cascade of efforts in Congress and [in] a succession of states to turn women into chattel, to shame them about sex and curb their reproductive rights," and the upcoming Fall 2012 election season. You can easily look up this column and read it yourself. Whether or not I always agree with her, Ms. Dowd is Master Writer and a ninja-turner-of-the-phrase, which is, indeed, why she gets paid by the NYT to hold forth on whatever she pleases. I want to highlight the images and phrases she used in this column that alarmed all my bells: "chastity belts," "Sex-retary of State," "humiliate," "penetrating," and finally "yoke" and "perversely" and "debase." When referring to Secretary Clinton, her word choices include "waltz," "compelling," "masterful," and "inevitable."

I would be remiss to not point out to you that I worked for Hillary Clinton's presidential campaign in 2008. It was a pivotal year in my life, in many of our lives. (If you care to read what my actual thoughts were back then, I have a blog post up on my website charmingly titled "Notes After The Election" or "Truth Like Sand In My Crotch.") I could only describe it in the aftermath as the awakening of my repressed ambition. It was not my ambition for my Self, though I had been struggling with that relationship for some time. It was bigger than that—a lioness'-yawning-maw ambition. It was an ambition I felt for all women, for all of humanity. For the first time in my life, I realized how badly I wanted a woman to be president. And I realized I hadn't even allowed myself to want it before, because I thought I couldn't have it. Defense Mechanisms 101.

Suddenly, in the form of Hillary Rodham Clinton, it was *possible*. I dared to hope. It changed me radically. That she lost the primary to Barack Obama also changed me. That he went on to win the election, and we received as a nation the healing gift of having our first President-of-color also changed me. I was overwrought, overjoyed; I embraced the elation, the magnitude of it. I then got to travel the entire emotional spectrum when I learned that Prop 8 had passed in the state of California, denying homosexuals the right to marry, a crushing and unexpected defeat. And then I quietly packed away my dream, though it would never quite fit back into its lock-box in my heart.

Now, the poem I wrote:

THE INEVITABLE GUARDIAN

The place inside me where my hopes live
is a long large bedroom, lined with many beds.
It is always morning. The light there is soft,
and whispers through the thin white curtains.
Most everyone is still dreaming,
though some have started to wake
and are surprised, like always,
when they blink their eyes open,
to be in not-dream, to be seeing.

The bedroom is in an orphanage,
which was a mansion in another lifetime,
which sits on a large estate of unwanted land.
There is no moat around the building.
There is no gate around the land.
It is unnecessary.
There are no visitors to ward off,
no intruders to question.
I've made sure of it. Or someone else did—
the original architect and his patron the landowner;
a government not-conspiracy of ignorance that built no roads;
some unchallenged law of physics.

So far, no one has tried to leave either.
There's only a few that have ever even sat up in their beds,
looked around, stretched. They're waiting
for something that has already happened
but hasn't happened yet.

There's only one that's ever spoken to me,
and only then to feverishly describe her dreams.

Today she tells me one she has told me a hundred times before.
We both know what she's going to say before she says it,
but she wants to tell it again, and I want to hear it.

I have arrived at a grand party
at a castle so impressive it makes breath hold its breath.
I am late. It is already very dark out.
I dressed in a gown, but it is covered in mud,
and I can't remember how it happened, how I got so dirtied.
How many fields did I pass over to get here on foot?
Were they swollen with so much rain? Was there quicksand?
Did the earth get hungry and swallow me?
Did I have to pull myself out alone?
Most of the mud has been dry for some time.
Was I buried in this dress, without even a coffin?
I am mortified. My face burns shame.
But remembering what my mother taught me about posture,
what I learned by pacing hallways with towers of books
stacked on my head, I stand up straight and I knock.

The Lady of the house opens the enormous door,
greets me exuberantly, takes no notice of the mud.
There is a light dancing around her head
that might be a trick of the chandeliers.
There are voices of many women and many champagne
glasses clinking and sparkling in the distance.
She smiles so warm and wide, she is suddenly familiar—
Is this a queen I've seen before in a photo of a painting? No, no.
Is this my great grandmother, who I have never seen
but am certain I would recognize? No, it's not her.
I search her face for an identity, but before I can find it,
she grabs me firmly by the hand and pulls me in from the night.
When she speaks, her voice is a song, like hearth fire is a broth,
like a precious metal pours itself generously in to the mold of a ring.
She says, "Where have you been Melinda?
We've all been waiting for you. Or do they call you Mindy now?
Never mind all that, Mind-eee," she exaggerates, and giggles,
a little tipsy, "never mind. Welcome home.
Come in. Come in."

SUMMARY:

- A great deal of poetry emerges from the nebulous, swirling emotions and thoughts that are unformed-yet-cloud-responses to things we've read, heard, seen, or experienced. There is something physically happening inside of us as we feel out these feelings and explore these thoughts. We are building floating electric railroad tracks between the islands, the discrete parts of our brains that store different kinds of information.

- Part of the way we build those literal, physical connections in our minds—those neuropathways—is with imagining new combinations of words and writing the phrases themselves.

- When we describe or name something, it has great power to change the thing itself. Try to understand and harness this power within you, and use that power for the good of the poem, and the good of your own mind. As Winifred Gallagher says in her book *Rapt: Attention and the Focused Life*, "Whatever your temperament, living the focused life is not about trying to feel happy all the time … Rather, it's about treating your mind as you would a private garden and being as careful as possible about what you introduce and allow to grow there." (This might be loosely related to pop-psychology on positive thinking, but we are light years past that over-simplification.)

- Remember we are Jungian sorcerers – use all the floating thoughts and feelings that are urgent in you right now and search out their connective tissue, the ways in which they are all pointing to the same meaning.

- Listen to music sometimes when you write. Not just for inspiration or to prompt a feeling-prompt. It is also extremely helpful should you get interrupted in the middle of a thought. You can quickly note what song you were listening to when you had to stop writing. When you have the chance to return to the piece, put that same music on again. It will help you recall where you were going with your thread, what the exact feeling or tone was. For incredibly in-depth information on why exactly this trick works, seek out the book This Is Your Brain On Music, by neuroscientist Daniel J. Levitin.

- Allow others' poems to inform and inspire your work. I might even go as far as saying that others' poetry should be your primary research material for generating new work.

- Don't forget to read newspapers and magazines, in print or online, and to stay alert to current topics and stories that fascinate you. History is happening right now.

- When seeking out a beginning for this kind of poem-jump-off, burn through to the thing that is scaring you the most about all of it. (Hello thesis!) For me, it was this clenched-heart-fear of hoping for things I may never have, my fear of the despair that might follow, my fear that I have a pivotal role to play in realizing my hopes —maybe even, uh god, a Responsibility—that I am not living up to. So I decided to start with my hopes and…(drum roll)

- Personify, *personify*, PERSONIFY: the fattest, raddest trick up our poet sleeves.

ASSIGNMENT

1. Make a list of ten things that are impossible.

2. Make a list of ten things that you do to celebrate, that give you incredible joy.

3. Now make a list of three things that are wrong in your world, or in the world, that you believe will never change, at least not soon or not even in your lifetime; their change is not impossible, but it is improbable to you. You have given up hope for them.

4. The title of your piece will be one the things from the second list happening, as in, "On The Day I Finally Forgave You" The rest of the piece will be a list poem where you make each of those impossible things also happen on that day. End the piece with some celebration.

CHAPTER 8: Architects of Yes

POEM CLIFF: STARTING FROM A STRUCTURE YOU WANT TO PLAY WITH

Another thing I have been feverishly obsessed with over the years is The Economy. Little known fact: I entered university as a Business and Economics major. That lasted all of one semester, during which I had the pleasure to take a class from the mayoral-looking Dr. Donald Booth—Intro to Macro or Micro Economics, I can't remember which. One day, with an attitude I can only describe as relish, Dr. Booth decided to prove definitively—using mathematic and economic models, in bright green marker on the dry erase board—why it would be better for the economy as a whole if women stayed home and men went to work to earn the family income. My initial shock lasted the kind of ten minutes that feels like ten years, and then I was furious. I raised my hand with objections, repeatedly. My fury only increased his relish. And that was the end of my potential career as an economist.

Other little known fact: for many years I worked in various capacities for the nonprofit Habitat for Humanity in fund development and communications. I was frequently sent out in slacks and blouses and pearls to pitch the VPs of corporations having anything to do with the housing industry: mortgage corporations, financial firms, major developers and construction companies, etc. It was my job to be attractive and enthusiastic and smiley, well-mannered and well-spoken, and to get them on board with donating to various low income housing projects Habitat had in the works. My job got harder and harder. Over those brief years, the donation coffers dwindled. Corporate belts were tightening in preparation for…what? I didn't know. But a market downturn was on the radar, and budgets for philanthropy were the first on the chopping block, naturally.

I had the chance one day after one of these meetings to have a semi-casual drink and chat with one such VP, and, a little loose from the 25-year-old Laphroaig, I dared to pose a query. I started, "I consider myself an intelligent girl" (if I had used the word "woman" there would have been scoffing), "but there's something about the mortgage finance industry I'm just not getting—the constant flipping of houses, the real estate valuations that regulate equity loans, the sheer volume of it all. How is it possible for the worth of property to keep sky-rocketing when the basic sticks and bricks value of property and houses seems like it should be pretty static, minus inflation or the massive gentrification of an area?" He laughed so hard, about $47 dollars worth of scotch came out his nose. He grabbed the closest white linen napkin to mop up his face and, with a big, proud-uncle smile responded, "You *are* a smart cookie, aren't you? Between you and me, it's all about to come crashing down. I'm converting my assets as we speak, mostly to gold. You should do the same." He says. To the girl who makes $28,000 a year for working 80-hours-a-week, who can't afford the median rental price on an apartment in the county she works in, but is giving daily speeches on the importance of home-ownership as a fundamental American value, a stabilizing force for families and thus, communities and society as a whole.

So let's just say I watched the epic financial system meltdown that began in the late-aughts, and the tax-payer-funded bailout that followed, and all the political episodes that would be the finishing touches on the canvas of Bush Jr.'s presidential legacy with relish. And fear. But not an ounce of surprise. Or, it turned out, Schadenfreude.

Quick shout out to Alex Blumberg and Adam Davidson and the whole team of reporters and producers at NPR's Planet Money and ProPublica who used every weapon in their communication arsenal to explain what created the economic apocalypse—derivatives, credit default swaps, CDOs and a mortgage-back-securities, and much much more. Clear enough so someone with only a semester of Macro (Micro?) Economics under her belt could Get It. And here's to Ira Glass and the whole crew at *This American Life* who featured *Planet Money*'s work continuously, leading to the opportunity for me to hear, straight from the mouth of Angelo Mozilo, CEO of the failed mortgage lender Countrywide, that "Nobody saw this coming."[18] Yes. *Nobody*. It was, as all the CEOs said repeatedly and practically in unison, an unpredictable perfect storm. Even Brian Moynihan from Bank of America testified before Congress, *under oath*, that, "No one involved in the housing systems, lenders, rating agencies, investors, insurers, consumers, regulators, or policy makers foresaw a dramatic and rapid depreciation in home prices."[18] To crib from Amy Poehler and Seth Meyers' Weekend Update mock-outrage-that-isn't segments on SNL, "Really, Brian? *Really?*"

It's been a fascinating three years since. Lately I've been drawn into researching more intensely the player that seemed to survive the "financial crisis" without a single scratch: Goldman Sachs. The stories I have absorbed about the history of this company, its leadership, and its *modus operandi* are, at this point, legion. But I was struck with great interest by the public resignation of Goldman Sach's executive Greg Smith, and his op-ed in the NYT, and the swift flurry of reaction to it in the papers and blogs. It so struck me, I started itching to enter the dialogue, you know, through poetry. AKA: how I enter the world.

When confronted by an idea and topic so massive as to be nearly unswallowable, I nearly always turn to my friend and yours, structure. I love playing with structures in creative writing. They solve SO many problems. I initially fell in love with structured writing not through a careful study of all the poetic forms that exist—sonnets, pantoums, villanelles—I don't know, there has to be more than a hundred established ones—but by a regular visitation to McSweeny's website and its Lists. If you don't know what I'm talking about, go now quick and Google it, and laugh your pantaloons off. It is the best education in playing with structure and form I can think to give you. Everything else I write from now on in this chapter might be moot.

The structure that came to me, before any of the concrete content ideas did, was the idea of a To-Do List of a CEO of a Major Financial Institution. What would that look like for real? Would he write it himself? (It's fair to assume it's a "he." An October, 2011 article in the USA Today titled "Number of Female 'Fortune' 500 CEOs at Record High" excitedly claimed that, if none of them stepped down before the end of the year, a record 18 women would be CEOs of the Fortune 500. That's getting dangerously close to 4%. Woohoo!) I thought, *no, why would he write his own to-do list? He probably has "people" for that.* So I expanded my structural idea to include that it would not just be a to-do list, but one transcribed by someone else.

This was really just for fun. What else am I to do with the rage boiling inside of me, threatening to cook my vital organs? I drew heavily from the research and notes I had taken on Goldman Sachs CEO and Board Chairman Lloyd Blankfein (though since the writing of this poem, and in reaction in part I am sure to the loss in stock-holder confidence since Greg Smith dropped his very personal, very relatable public relations atom bomb, Forbes has just reported that a Solomon-esque decision has been made at Goldman Sachs to separate the role of CEO from the role of Chairman of the Board, with Lloyd getting the Board Chairman half of the baby.[19]). But I also feel that the pattern of behavior displayed by the executives at Goldman Sachs is exactly that—a pattern. One that is woven throughout the fabric of Wall Street. Trying to decipher the real differences in corporate cultures amongst the several major-player firms can be like trying to figure out the real differences between, say, two religious denominations, one who insists communion be taken every week and the other only once a month. Which I hear is a REALLY big difference, and I should stop being so irreverent and disrespectful.

Before I share the structure-exercise poem that came out of all this, I am also just dying to share the fact that, in the process of this research, I found my favorite Internet blog comment ever. It was left on the very informative blog, "Good Morning Silicon Valley," in a post titled *Quoted: on Goldman Sachs op-ed*, which quoted Whitney Tilson, founder of hedge fund T2 Partner, responding to Greg Smith's public resignation in the NYT by saying, "What's the next 'shocking' headline: 'Prostitution in Vegas!?'" But that's not my favorite. My favorite comment ever can only be attributed to the mysterious username Bryan. He wrote: "Reared on the fantasy of their own eternal entitlement, systematically deprived of education, sated on corn syrup and beer, and propagandized 24/7, Americans are now arguably the most passive population of human beings the world has ever seen. Are you incapable of anger, or merely of action? What part of 'hang a few admirals' do y'all fail to understand?"[20] Amen, whoever you are, amen.

Now here's the poem already:

TO–DO–LIST OF A CEO OF A MAJOR FINANCIAL INSTITUTION, AS TRANSCRIBED BY HIS ADMINISTRATIVE ASSISTANT, WHO HAS A WATER-TIGHT CONFIDENTIALITY CLAUSE THAT INCLUDES LEGAL REPERCUSSIONS FOR HER GREAT GRAND-CHILDREN

1. Call Forbes editor personally. Tell him to eat fifty dicks.

2. Call White House and Treasury department about weekly meeting; ask to move to Tuesdays.

3. Follow up on the recruiting of that brilliant young scientist—what was his name? The one who thinks he can cure cancer? Need him on board for inventing new algorithms for capitalizing on all likely massive earthquakes in next decade. CC that to CFO—compensation NO OBJECT.

4. Get VP of Corporate Communications on plan to regain Guinness Book of World Records title for world's largest hug.

    a. Sub-note on previous two action items: get guy at NSA on the phone about starting application process for using their Earthquake Machine. Find if possible to take down those insurgent assholes in Ayacucho, Peru. Get General Alexander to expedite, and ask him if we can move back Saturday's golf game to 9am.

5. Tell Linda to pen a thank you note to Walter. Make sure she uses the phrases "great strategic mind" and "excellent taste in double malts." He'll eat that up. Solicit his further advice on execution of plan to plant publicity attacking me and asking me to step down; will rile up

the Board; they won't want to appear weak or beholden to media; will postpone them asking for my resignation for at least 5 years. Genius.

6. Look up all antonyms for "toxic," "destructive," and "callous." Forward to PR Department.

7. Remind Jenny to follow up with that hot young Scandinavian artist about commission for golden parachute sculpture made of gold for third summer home; connect her with Zuma's people and tell her he said, "no problem."

8. Consider moving minimum-interview requirement for new hires from 6 to 8. 6 doesn't feel intimidating enough anymore; sheep are getting through that aren't sheepish enough.

9. Saw that unbearable bitch from the Energy and Power Group wearing flats and her hair down again. She was laughing with someone on the phone. Alert HR to red flag, get the removal paperwork started.

10. Google "inflation and why it's bad," summarize it and forward to me. Not sure what the Tim-ster was talking about.

11. Mail birthday card to Ben Bernanke; encrypt code in it for this year's Swiss account; update him on progress we've made locating family heirlooms acquired by the Nazis.

12. Order more fresh lion meat.

Rather than dig into any analysis of why I picked the content I did, and chose the tone of voice I did, I would rather just point out other ways I could have handled this exact same topic, with punch-drunk zeal. I would rather just try to directly transfer to you the total heart-on I have for playing with structure in poetry by demonstrating how flexible and endless the possibilities are with this tactic. So, a list of other structures I could have chosen to play with to get this poem off my chest:

• A bored high-school student's 5-paragraph essay on the op-ed "Why I Am Leaving Goldman Sachs" that was an assignment for a Junior-year Social Studies class.

• An outrageous, hilarious grocery list written by a caterer for a Goldman Sachs Board of Directors weekend retreat in Southampton.

- A Gawker-style rant to all the employees of these firms, who are complicit in the destruction of the very fabric of society when they follow the directives to put the firms profit margins over the interests of the clients and lie blatantly to them in the process. À la Hamilton Nolan's rant, "You Are Not Going to Win the Lottery, You Fool."[21]

- A list poem of rejected Goldman Sachs Holiday Party ideas.

- The Constitution of The United States, as rewritten by Lloyd Blankfein.

- The scripted conversation a Goldman Sachs VP has every Friday night with his weekly hired prostitute, who he insists wears a cream Chanel suit and responds to his mother's name, "Beverly." (Too dark? Nope. Not since the NYT published its expose "Financers and Sex Trafficking," by Nicholas D. Kristof on April 1, 2012.)

- April Fools Day pranks to play on a Goldman Sachs new-hire that put their new non-sense-of-humor-about-Goldman-Sachs to the test.

- Names for new Economics Models proving the rich deserve to get richer at the expense of the working poor because it's better for all of us, titled *Trickling Downer*.

- Instructions for Cat's Cradle moves, or yoga moves, which are also named after the power connections discovered by studying the map on Muckety. com, where it is revealed that Goldman Sachs International has direct or once-removed relationships with 493 people, organizations or other entities in its database of the most influential people in America.

I could go on. But I'll let you take it from here.

SUMMARY:

- Structure is your friend. (Also see: Chapter 5, "restrictions can be very helpful.")

- When you are facing especially dark or dense or complex source material, structure can ground you totally, and give you brilliant ideas for disarming points of entry.

- That last part—where I brought up the word "disarming"? This is a big idea I want you to grab hold of, real tight. Disarming the reader with humor, or irony, or absurdity, or playfulness—this is how you get them to drop to their guard so you can get the punch of Dark Truth or Uncomfortable Wisdom in. (Secret bonus knowledge: this is also how you disarm yourself.)

- Let the news inspire you! Read the news, in some form, on a regular basis. If a story sticks to your insides, get into full truffle-pig research mode. Dig and dig and dig; sniff and sniff and smell. There is something valuable, and you're going to find it.

- Don't be afraid to get topical and NOW. Don't be stymied by a bogus belief that everything you write has to be timeless. Poems can be grounded in a place and a time in history, in pop culture, and yes, some people might not get it, not now nor in the future, because they will not have the background information necessary to understand what you are talking about. Who cares! Make them do the research! Or screw 'em!

- Don't be afraid to get dense! Not every topic is Euclidean geometry. Some topics are quantum-mechanics-complex. Some of the best poems are perfectly distilled and simple and brief, and use ten words to mean ten thousand words. But others are epic, sprawling, and ambitious; they are so dense they keep growing in density even after they are written.

- Borrow structural ideas from everything and everywhere. Keep a list of structures you think it would be fun to explore someday.

- Have FUN. Seriously.

ASSIGNMENT

Structure really is your best friend. The trick is to match up a topic you want to write about with a potential structure that will be your point of entry, and then adding a twist. Your assignment is to pick a topic, something with personal emotional charge, and write about it in at least five different ways using completely different structures.

SOME WRITING STRUCTURES:	FOR EXAMPLE:
How-to instructions	Let's say you want to write about a recent break-up.
Recipes	
A desert island list	Maybe tell the story of an argument that led to a break-up in the form of an anti-desert island list? (Call the poem Torture Island, imagine five things from that relationship you would never want to be stranded with.)
Series of "I statements"	
A personal ad	
A resume	
Home Shopping Network pitch	Maybe tell it in the form of footnotes referencing earlier arguments?
Rock song (chorus/verse/chorus/verse/ bridge/chorus…)	Maybe write the story of your doomed relationship straight, and in chronological order; then reverse it, so that the poem ends in the first time you met?
Chronology or timeline	
Police report on a crime scene	
Footnotes	Maybe dash out a quick food-critic-style review of your famous last words in your last big argument, how you could have added more expletives and the appetizers lacked foreshadowing? Give it a cheeky name, like "Is revenge best served cold?"
Pros and cons list	
Shopping list	
Food critic's review	
Invented (or actual) band names	Maybe write a resume of all your failed relationships as if they were places you worked and developed certain skills?
Pick up lines	
Names of yoga positions or dance moves	
New Year's resolutions	Maybe make a list of yoga moves named after all the compromises you made over the years to stay together?
Greeting card messages	
A politician's public apology	
Last will and testament	
Madlibs	

CHAPTER 9: ACHILLES HEELING

POEM CLIFF: STARTING FROM A VULNERABILITY

I was inspired recently by a phone conversation with poet Brian Ellis, who had an upcoming workshop he was teaching. I asked him what his plan was, and his response was one of the best workshop ideas I had ever heard. He wanted to share with the attendees his obsession with playing with technological mediums in writing. He planned to have them write the same poem three times, and rotate every ten minutes amongst the three technological mediums he would have there—pen and paper, typewriter, and computer. This sprang loosely from something he had long known about and that had captured his imagination—that fiction didn't arrive until after the printing press had been invented. He believed the relationship between content and medium was fascinating. He had never even *read* Marshal McLuhan. Brian's mind is the best.

So then I asked, "So what's the writing prompt?" And he replied, "Pick one of your greatest vulnerabilities and imagine it as your roommate in a small two bedroom apartment." GAH-ZING! I was floored. My only comment was, "You better give those folks some time to think about and write down three of their vulnerabilities *before* you drop that prompt on their heads. It might be really rough for some of them."

One of my greatest vulnerabilities is my need to receive the benefit of the doubt from people. When I don't get it, especially from anyone I consider a friend, new and improved Richter Scales sprout from my head. I'm saying I lose my shit like a 15-year-old girl. It ruins everything for me. And it terrifies me, how this one value I have can wreck so much havoc on my emotions, my mind and my relationships. It might be my softest spot, if not my Achilles' Heel.

I was given the great gift of compassion for myself on this issue after reading an important essay by the esteemed author Rebecca Solnit, titled "Men Explain Things to Me," and then subtitled, "Facts Didn't Get in Their Way." It was written and published in 2008. It is, in part, a diatribe about the many men she has met who have diminished, ignored or held forth over her, and that "the out-and-out confrontational confidence of the totally ignorant is, in my experience, gendered. Men explain things to me, and other women, whether or not they know what they're talking about. Some men."[22] But it is an essay about something much bigger than the struggle to cope with arrogance. After tying in and commenting on the Bush Administration's famous arrogance and the war we went to in Iraq over nonexistent WMDs, she writes eloquently:

> Arrogance might have had something to do with the war, but this syndrome is a war that nearly every woman faces every day, a war within herself too, a belief in her superfluity, an invitation to silence, one from which a fairly nice career as a writer (with a lot of research and facts correctly deployed) has not entirely freed me…

> Don't forget that I've had a lot more confirmation of my right to think and speak than most women, and I've learned that a certain amount of self-doubt is a good tool for correcting, understanding, listening, and progressing — though too much is paralyzing and total self-confidence produces arrogant idiots, like the ones who have governed us since 2001. There's a happy medium between these poles to which the genders have been pushed, a warm equatorial belt of give and take where we should all meet.

> More extreme versions of our situation exist in, for example, those Middle Eastern countries where women's testimony has no legal standing; so that a woman can't testify that she was raped without a male witness to counter the male rapist. Which there rarely is.

> **Credibility is a basic survival tool.** [22]

That bolding and italicizing of that last line, "Credibility is a basic survival tool," was mine, not hers. The moment I read that line something sighed deeply within me. She gave me the phrase I needed so that I could understand why credibility, or benefit of the doubt, was so high stakes for me. Why it made me feel so vulnerable. At a real level, this was about my very survival.

So I sat down and did a little free-associating about this vulnerability of mine, mostly in my own head, and a little bit on paper. For some reason, it came up for me in a very vivid, nagging way that I had just been contacted by a man who I shared my third-grade class with. He had attended a show the year before that I had performed at in Iowa City at the Mission Creek Festival, because he had read my name in the paper, and thought there couldn't possibly be another one of me. That he even remembered my name after all these years was like protein to a blood-sugar crash. (Hi, Nick Caster! If you're reading this, you're the best!) We had the chance to hang out a bit that night and, because he had stayed in Iowa, he was able to catch me up on what had happened to anyone I could remember (including that my first crush, the lisping twin Matt of a boy named Pat had become an investment banker or something on Wall Street. Egads.) We both spoke with near-to-tears reverence about our 3rd grade teacher, Mrs. Patton.

She was truly the greatest teacher I would ever have, certainly in the first ten years of my public school education. My most powerful memory of her is the day her dog died, and she got the call at her desk in front of all of us, and rather than hide it, or run out of the classroom to unleash her grief, she told us all what had happened and burst into tears. That she would be so vulnerable in front of us was something I had never seen an adult do, not with that kind of grace and openness. Oh, Mrs. Patton. The things I learned from you!

Nick put something in beautiful perspective for me in his last email, where he wrote, "For some reason, third grade seems like the last year I was really a kid, and that seems significant." He also reminded me of the name of our student teacher that year, Mr. Ellis. Is anyone else already hearing/feeling the synchronicity gongs going off? So, I started writing, and this is what came of it:

THE THING I WILL NEVER REALLY UNDERSTAND, NO MATTER HOW MUCH I KNOW

I. BEGINNING
I was absent from class the day our 3rd grade student teacher,
Mr. Ellis, flush with young ambition,
gave a lesson on Prejudice.

I showed up the next day to a simple quiz:
"Name three groups of people who are likely to experience prejudice."
I had never heard or read the word before. I panicked quietly.
I glanced at my neighbor's paper, where he had written:
1. blacks
2. women
3. gays

What did *that* mean?
My neighbor Nicole was the giggliest girl I knew.
When she smiled it was like soft quartz secrets
were bubbling out of her. She was black.
I was a woman, or I would be someday, and so would my sisters,
and my mother was definitely a woman.
My father was gay—would we all get prejudice?
Was it a sickness?

I copied down the answers, being sure to switch the order a bit,
and turned my paper in when the others did,
and the rest of the day I tensed with fear of getting yanked
by my invisible leash to the teacher's desk after class,
and delivered the punishment that I deserved.

II. DIGRESSION

The only other time I had cheated was the year before,
in the 2nd grade, during Creative Writing Time,
where I passed off most of what I could remember of a poem
about a mouse named Nora as my own work.
Sure, some words had changed,
but the story was pure seven-year-old plagiarism:

A young mouse named Nora was very clumsy, and exuberant,
and was always dancing around and singing at the top of her lungs
and running in the house and breaking things, a total ruckuser,
and her mother was always shaming her for making TOO MUCH NOISE.

I was never caught then either, though I had been positive
that at Parent Night my mother would open up my portfolio of work,
see the Noisy Nora poem, and frown at me with foreshadowed rage.
My mother either didn't see the poem, or didn't recognize
it's similarity to a book from our messy home library,
or didn't care. She beamed at me the whole night.

III. UNDIGRESSION

I ran home from the bus that afternoon
and went straight for the heavy red dictionary,
flipped through to the "P"s, the "Pr"s, then the "Pre"s, then—
there it was:

prejudice
prej-u-dice [prej-*uh*-dis]
-noun
1. opinion formed beforehand or without knowledge
2. unreasonable, hostile attitudes regarding a group
-verb (used with object) – diced –dicing
3. to affect with prejudice

This cleared up nothing for me.
Why would anyone be hostile towards "blacks, women, gays"?
I had missed a very important lesson.
I was too scared and embarrassed to ask the adults to explain.
I was going to have to figure it out on my own.

I want to point out that I have never shared that story of my early poetic plagiarism with anyone, *ever*. Writing it down now, it's so obviously harmless, and innocent, and hardly deep-dark-secret-worthy. (Real talk: I was six-years-old. For a six-year-old that is bury-it-in-the-backyard-before-you-get-caught-and-whacked-with-a-wooden-spoon scary.) And beyond that, I think in writing it I have discovered something important, a key to a lock on a door I didn't even know was there. My shame about that incident, my fear of being found out as the fraud I really was, ensured I would never, ever do that again. It is entirely possible, I am now seeing, that my reticence about studying poetry formally in college, or attending workshops in general, can be traced back to this small, seemingly insignificant early trauma. Or that my defensiveness about being given the benefit of the doubt comes straight from my over-corrections to these early feelings of being a fraud.

This is what we're here for, what this manifesto is about. This is what the work of writing poetry makes possible—accessing in ourselves the stories behind the stories behind the stories. We can burn through not just to "First Thoughts," but to First Experiences—the origins of our beliefs, our behavior, our programming; the stuff we wake up every day with and allow to conduct us like blind, dumb marionettes in our own lives. The writing and free-associating eventually reveals the origins we are terrified to face because they might mean something Big and they might Change us, and we can't know what we will be like on the other side of that Change. We might not be masters of our fates after all, or we might have been all along. Is this what is meant by "self-fulfilling prophecies"?

I hope this happens for you, too, as you invent and explore and execute your own writing exercises. I hope you discover memories that were once dormant, and suddenly come alive and bright as light bulbs being switched on, illuminating the dark recesses of your Self. I hope you dog those memories, watch their every move closely and with bated breath. I hope specifically that any of them you have buried purposefully out of shame or embarrassment are allowed to come out of hiding, roam about, play. Watch the play. It created you. It is creating you. It has birthed your biases, your truths, your perceptions—the windows through which you see everything, *feel* everything that has happened or is happening to you.

Talk to the memories. (I mean that only literally if you're into Gestalt.) Wait, why am I parenthesizing Gestalt? Gestalt is just another way of doing exactly what we are doing. The three main rules of the phenomenological exploration called Gestalt therapy are (1) epoché, (2) description, and (3) horizontalization. That's psychobabble for (1) setting aside one's biases and prejudices in order to suspend expectations and assumptions, (2) describing as opposed to *explaining*, and (3) giving each thing that comes up, each "item of description" an equal value or significance.[23]

So talk to the memories, the ideas that come up for you. Dialogue with them, either on paper or out loud like a crazy person. (These days, people will probably just think you're on your cell phone.) They will answer all your questions about why you do the things you do, why you make the choices you make, why you treat people the way you do, why you cook your soup like that. *How you do anything is how you do everything.*

SUMMARY:

- Build relationships with other writers. Talk to them frequently. Take a great interest in their process and work. They have a lot of juicy inspirado for you.

- Aside to the first point: writers you admire are not, I promise you, living in golden temples built on the edges of volcanoes on Venus. They are not lounging in plush velveted salons in said temples, enrobed in silk smoking jackets, sipping Venutian scotch, holding forth on existentialism for a handful of acolytes they had rocketed to outer space for the privilege of being their personal drooling audience. They are relatively normal people (on the artist spectrum of normal). They *are* probably busy, because they have, you know, lives, and work, and deadlines, and families, and problems. But I am saying they are not Venus-inaccessible. Look them up! Write to them. Let them know you love their work. Ask them questions about their writing, or about writing in general. They might write back.

- As Natalie Goldberg says, and it always bears repeating: *go for the jugular.* Get that pen-sword out and cut through to where the blood will be sure to gush. Writing about your vulnerabilities is a guaranteed glittery blood bath.

- Self-doubt is an important tool. Nearly all the artists I know are, from time to time, if not all the time, battling being crippled by self-doubt. Self-confidence is also an important tool, but can be just two clicks away from arrogance. Seek balance. Balance does not imply that you find a centered position and stay there indefinitely. It implies that things are always shifting beneath you, and you need to correct and adjust and move so as not to fall down. As Ms. Solnit put it, find that "warm equatorial belt of give and take."

- I'm going to keep saying it: FREE ASSOCIATE. Let your mind wander all over the place. Follow whatever emerges that has the Charge. And follow anything and everything that shows up to the party already wearing the Crown of Synchronicity.

- Part of writing poetry, and certainly publishing it or performing it, is about being vulnerable, publically, and learning to cope with it gracefully. Let's all aspire to be Mrs. Pattons on this one. Your willingness to let other people see your places of greatest pain and weakness models what strength in vulnerability looks like, teaches them compassion, empowers them.

- Use cantos or poem-sections if you feel like it! It's very Kerouac! It's a great way to make it look like you totally planned to veer off course entirely all along. And maybe you did. It also gives you more potential titles! More opportunities to plant meaning! Yeah!

- When you sit down to write, and in life in general, suspend your disbelief.

- Talk to your memories. They invented your soft spots, and are experts on a lot of things. Like the assumptions hiding beneath your assumptions. Ask them questions. Listen to what they have to say.

ASSIGNMENT

Remember the first time (or the last time) you tried to be "cool" and failed miserably. How old were you? Were you trying to impress someone? What were the circumstances? What did you do to try to affect "cool"? Did you change your appearance? Pretend to know about something you know nothing about? What happened?

This might not seem like it at first, but this prompt gets right to the heart of a near-universal human vulnerability: the need for people to like us or love us or see us in a certain way we don't think they will already see us.

This can be written in first, second, or third person. It can also be about someone else that you know and love who did something wildly not-them to impress someone.

CHAPTER 10:
Oh, The Places You've Been

POEM CLIFF: STARTING FROM A PLACE YOU HAVE LIVED AND HAD VIVID EXPERIENCES IN

I might love the word "vivid" even more than "nebulous." Maybe just because of the "v"s. I love "v"s. Can't get enough of them. But my word-crush probably has more to do with the fact that it's a small word (only two v-filled syllables!) that calls up such big bright things. No—not big and bright; *too* big, *too* bright. Things that pulse with energy and assault and overwhelm the senses. Things you have to squint at. Things that bring you to your knees. Life in full neon.

We started these chapters on writing with me convincing you that nothing is too dull to be writer-magicked into a poem. But the trick of getting the dull to shine, we now know, is by connecting it to the vivid. We free associate until we get gripped by something pulsing with life. Then we search out the connections. The ceiling fan becomes the soft drumming air of portent, becomes the soundtrack to the summer you started stealing and had to practice being quiet. The rotting fruit in your fridge gets Richard-Brautiganed into a funeral parlor makeup drawer. The inanimate objects around us are just waiting to be seen in a different light. They are familiar, but they are not dull. (They may not even be inanimate. Tom Robbins covered this territory in *Skinny Legs And All* so I don't have to.)

The places we live are rich with source treasure, but can also suffer from "your-own-backyard" syndrome. You live somewhere long enough and the wide eyes of the tourist are routined right out of you. You are no longer shocked by your neighbors, the deaf twins, having another silent fight in the courtyard. You become annoyed by the movie theater that dominates all the street parking on Rocky Horror Nights. You walk the same paths repeatedly. You are bored with the weather.

If this is how you feel about the place you live right now, you are doing something terribly wrong. SNAP OUT OF IT! The places we live in and visit are not just the settings to the dramas or minutiae of our lives. They are characters themselves. They are catalysts. Writing about them can do so much more then set a scene: how you choose to describe a place can say everything about the action that took place there, without you having to tell "what happened" at all. Your list of things-to-write-about should include all the places you've lived and been, whether they are entire cities or cramped apartments. And now I'm just stalling.

★ ★ ★

We've arrived, dear readers, at the hardest chapter for me to write. I've got tissues, a hot cup of tea, a toasted hoodie on fresh from the dryer. The Yeah Yeah Yeah's *It's Blitz* has been playing softly. I don't know if it's enough.

The poem I wrote for this chapter was written in 25 minutes on a plane flight to Long Beach. But the event that generated it happened on Valentine's Day 2001, when I fell in love very suddenly. Let me rephrase: I fell in LOVE like an ancient iron hammer to the head. Like a shot of liquid LSD to the heart, like the way only a first real love can set off the dopamine-serotonin-norepinephrine-oxytocin chorus to perform the entire Sondheim catalogue in your blood. I am so, so sorry if this has not happened to you yet. And I am also so jealous; I could die wanting to be you.

The relationship that started that day lasted for nearly 10 years, and its story does not belong to anyone but us. I will not tell it here. Pieces of it will shine through, I'm sure, directly and indirectly, in poems I write for the rest of my life. But as I write this, it has been sixteen months since I left, *only six months* after a commitment ceremony on sacred land in Ojai, California, beneath a thousand-year-old oak tree. The ceremony itself was bizarre and colorful, and included a series of physical challenges we had invented to complete together, including karate punching boards with our hands red-ribbon-tied together, splitting a Moroccan geode in half, the old German tradition of sawing a log (I am so sorry I risked your life for that one, Ben Rojas) and, finally, shooting bottles, two single ones and then one together, with our pink and brown BB guns. It was so joyous and beautiful and perfect. After we kissed, we walked off into the sunset with our guns slung on our backs to the applause of our family and friends and Karen O's song, "All Is Love," from the *Where the Wild Things Are* soundtrack playing.

I still can't listen to that song. Maybe after I finish this book, I'll give it a shot.

When I left that relationship, I left the only home, the only stability, the only comfort I had ever known. The reasons are many and personal, but suffice it to say, for an entire decade that love was the greatest distraction I had ever known. I would not take the risks I needed to take in my life so that I might follow my crazy dream of being a poet for a living. I worried so constantly about taking care of us, tending to our bond, and keeping our house intact and our rent and bills paid. It concerned and occupied me above all else.

The succession of events that led me to the decision to leave were epic, Shakespearean, Tom Robbinsian, Diane DiPrimal. When the thought first planted itself in my mind, *you could leave*, it was so overwhelming I could not hold it in my head for longer than five seconds at a time. How could I break the heart I had protected, and poured all my magic into for ten years? What kind of person would that make me? What would my family think of me? What would my friends think of me? How could they even look at me if I did this? Would I become hardened and bitter with shame and regret? All for what? Some delusion of destiny? For poetry?

A word had haunted me for months prior: Integrity. What did it mean, to have it? Surely it meant more than a mechanical keeping of promises. If this were my only life, if I only had a short time left in it, what did I really want to do? What did I really value above all else? Honesty? Poetry? Loyalty? What kind of life was this that required these impossible choices? What did I need more—the love and respect of others, or my own? What consequences could I survive to protect what I was discovering were the most valuable things to me—my freedom, my imagination, my love of poetry?

I had also been going through this whole face-all-my-fears-one-by-one thing for at least a year. I thought my greatest fear was of committing, of marrying, because my parents' marriage had ended so tragically, with nervous breakdowns and mental illness, with poverty, with suicide attempts, with an enduring pain and existential confusion for my parents and my sisters and I. But! Aha! As it turned out, my greatest fear was not of getting married, becoming someone's wife, though that was in the top ten greatest fear hits. My Greatest Fear was of divorce. What family karmic patterns had I been blindly playing out to exorcise those demons?

I will be unpacking this for many many years to come, struggling to forgive myself for this transgression. And I don't mean intellectualized forgiveness—"knowing" I made the right choice for me, embracing self-compassion, and letting go of my guilt. I mean deep, hidden reservoir emotional resolution. I still feel heavy shame on the regular about "what I did."

Thank you, by the way, for hanging in there with me through this therapy session. I haven't been able to talk or write about it much, not really, not beyond the poem I wrote in its immediate aftermath, because I had a feature booked that week at the Ugly Mug in Orange, and I NEVER miss a show unless there's illness, death, dismemberment or acts of God involved. And also, I'll let you in on a small secret of mine—I kind of *love* performing in the middle of a nervous breakdown. Is there any better catharsis? I did not want to have to answer anyone's questions since, thanks to the speed of online social-networks and the old-fashioned telephone-tree rumor mill, people had HEARD. So I wrote a poem called "What Happened" and read it that night. I don't remember reading it. I probably cried. I probably made the audience cry.

And then there was THE AFTERMATH. I had to pack up everything I owned before Christmas and put it in storage. I spent the next ten-and-a-half months on the road, either performing in shows or producing them. How I managed to imagine, organize and execute all that work during a year of crushing, paralyzing grief, I can't really explain. Except to say I had no choice. I needed to earn money so I could afford to move away from Long Beach, from the scene of my crimes, where every coffee shop, every bar, every park, every sidewalk whispered *what you did, what you did, what you did.*

I reached out to one of my oldest friends in life and poetry—the aforementioned Rachel McKibbens, whom I had met at a poetry show hosted at a bar called the Que Sera, and who had lived a thousand lives since then. We created a show called The Last Nerve: A High Tea Poetry Brawl, wrote some intentionally feminist poetry and bits to anchor the production and sharpen our pitch to colleges with Women's Studies Programs and, well, because it was who we *were* and where we were *at*. On our last nerve. The show, the tour, ITS continuing aftermath have been, to say the least, transformational for me, personally. And despite my emotional apocalypse, or perhaps, I can admit, *because of it*, I've gotten more work done creatively and professionally in the last sixteen months than the last sixteen years combined. Shout out to the warm embrace of workaholism when times are dark.

On my recent trip back "home" from Portland to Long Beach, I realized something even bigger—it was my deep love for my family, and not just my ex, that had been, and continues to be my greatest distraction. When I am near them, I just want to love them, in all its verbiness. I want to fix my mom's computer. I want to be there emotionally for my sister while she grapples with new motherhood. I want to babysit my niece. I want to help my dad crawl out of every frustrating hole he falls into. Etcetera. I need to be physically, geographically distant from them for awhile, just so I can get all this work done, so I can finish this particularly meaty chunk of my self-actualization. At the very least, I needed to go away for awhile so I could have the time and emotional space to get the kind of deep-cave-feral-writer-animal this book has required me to become. I often joke that I smell like Balance Bars right now. But I am totally NOT joking.

Deep breath.

★ ★ ★

I am very lucky when it comes to plane-row neighbors, and neighbors in general—seriously, ridiculously lucky. One time, on a flight back to Los Angeles from Oahu, I sat next to my pre-assigned stranger, settled my stuff, turned to my right, and introduced myself. I nearly always do this. I'm going to clock it at 92% of the time, and always *always* if the flight is going to be a long one.

The stranger, it turns out, was a composer from Switzerland, but who spent at least half of his youth in Massachusetts. He had the aura of European about him, but spoke flawless American English like only a Massachusettsian can. We exchanged brief histories: he was studying at a conservatory in Boston, on his way back there from a wedding; I was a poet, on my way home from GirlFest. Our conversation flowed instantly and easily, and we were both energized to be sitting next to a fellow artist. At one point during the flight, he saw my book—*Rise of the Trust Fall*—sticking out of my bag, and asked if he could take a look. I obliged. He opened it to a random page and read who-knows-what and sighed richly and contentedly. Then he closed the book, examined the cover, and suddenly burst into a private fit of joy. "What is *happening* to you?" I asked, smiling wide. He said, "Do you know what your last name means?" I said, "No, I don't. I don't even know if it's French or German." Then he dropped the most delicious candied bomb. "Your name is German. It's from an old dialect in the Southern regions." (Side note: I am so embarrassed when hanging out with Europeans, who, in my experience, are more likely than not to be fluent in *more* than five languages, compared to me and my 1.5.) He went on, "Nettifee literally translates to Nice Fairy. You're Glinda the Good Witch! I knew it!" At this point in the book, I don't have to explain to you what this information did to me. Oh my stars, oh my luck.

On my most recent flight to Long Beach, my neighbor ended up being a JetBlue pilot. I'm not going to describe him or our exchange, because it's all in the poem, but suffice to say the moment he went to sleep I wrote feverishly and messily. And this is what I wrote. It's a letter to Amelia Earhart.

ASSUME CRASH POSITIONS

It's been almost 75 years Amelia.
They're breathing new life into the mystery of your disappearance—
some US-South Pacific public relations campaign stunt—
but the pilot sitting next to me on my flight to Long Beach

assures me they'll never find you, or Fred Noonan.
"The South Pacific," he says, "I've flown over it myself.
It's just too big." You just ran out of fuel, he tells me.
Your downfall was your communication skills,
your weakness with the radio.

I'm sitting next to him because I sprang
for the extra exit row dough on a whim, a whopping $35.
I think we're the only row on the plane without a middle-seat passenger.
I don't play scratch cards, but I imagine this is what winning $35 feels like.
He's got three flights later—from Long Beach to Seattle,
from Seattle to Long Beach, then Long Beach to Portland.
He's flying to his flights.
He has ear plugged his ears and closed his eyes
and fallen into sleep instantly,
or some deep pilot zazen trance.

Just ten minutes ago we were chatty aunts.
I told him I was a poet,
which always feels like I'm admitting I mime for a living.
He told me was the grandson of the famous songwriter,
the one who wrote "Back In The Saddle Again."
He told me he wrote songs, too,
and his best ones came to him while he lived on Oahu.
I told him my favorite Oahu memory—
jumping out of a plane over the North Shore,
how I fell through a rainbow disc in a cloud,
how I'd never realized rainbows were circles.
He told me his father was a gunman in the Second World War,
and had to jump out of a plane when it caught on fire.
His father told him that story and it lit his imagination.
He took his first solo flight when he was ten.
He was hooked.

You were ten when you saw your first plane at an Iowa State Fair.
I read that somewhere, and that you were called Millie.
I cut into my first geode in Iowa, Millie.
It made me want to slice into everything hard
and find the jewelry inside of it.
You made your first flight from Long Beach, where I'm headed.
It is the most home I've ever known,
though I've disappeared now, too.
I am in constant flight.

Nowhere is home but what I carry inside of me.
Did you feel that way too?
Let's leave all that at radio silence.
I don't want to picture you floating speechless
in the great big Lost. I prefer every other picture
I've seen of you—casually brave, flirting for the cameras.

In the exit rows of passenger planes these days,
everything is stickered with pictogram instructions
of what to do in the event of an event. You aren't allowed
to sit in an exit row without giving a verbal YES
that you are willing to help should the worst happen.
There are other criteria: you must speak English.
You must recognize fire, smoke, water, general signs of danger.
You must be able-bodied enough to open the door
and assist other passengers off the plane.
I pull out the laminated Information Safety Card
from the seatback pocket. It's the first one I've ever seen
that doesn't have the photo of the woman in the water,
the one calmly hugging her flotation cushion to her chest,
her hair awash, her face expressionless as death.

I've always liked that woman.
It's like no matter how many times her plane goes down,
she's ready to float. It's like she lives there,
in the wide open blue. It's like she's at home.
I wish she were here now, in this card.
Where did she go?
Why has she disappeared?

Just a few interesting additional process notes on this piece. For many years,
when I was younger, I stole Information Safety Cards from every flight I took.
I had a thing back then for committing small federal crimes, acts I considered
relatively harmless vandalisms, like removing the gas caps from Mail trucks.
(Remember THAT Paul Mathers?) These acts were just me pulling a
psychological safety valve, releasing the pressure of my adolescent angst and
rage and powerlessness, all the things I felt about the biggest authority in my
life: The Government. The Government, I felt, was nothing more than an
organized conspiracy of petty deceit and major disinformation intent on and
threatening to succeed at turning the American voting populace into nothing
more than uneducated, complacent, self-destructive sheep at the mercy and

service of the Rich and the Powerful. (See: the collected works of George Orwell, Philip K. Dick, Ray Bradbury and Aldous Huxley, among others.) (See also: the history of all empires.)

I still have a huge stash of those cards somewhere. They've always seemed important to keep, even if just for the entertainment value of seeing the pictogramage evolve to include walkmans (those were portable audio cassette players, for anyone super-young who is reading this), cell phones, laptops, iPods, handheld game consoles, mini-DVD players, etc. And I was always obsessed with the pictogram of the floating woman. I used her as my cover art for an early chapbook entitled *Flotation Cushion*. The ways in which my past is constantly informing my present is endlessly fascinating to me. We've discussed this at length already.

The reason this was the hardest chapter for me to write is not just because the poem and its process-explication required revealing to you some intense and private suffering over the past two years. It also has to do with the general topic at hand: the connections we have to places, to the geographical scenes of our lives. In the immortal words of Anaïs Nin, "We don't see things as they are but as we are." We project onto these places all of our psychological relief maps.

I am in Not-Long-Beach right now, not because I don't love that city, or the people in it and near it. I just can't handle being there right now, as I endure this long stretch of grief cycling, which after my six adult years living there, my one year of being a teenager there, the extreme joys and tragic failures of my most significant love-relationship-to-date having taken place there… well, I'm just not going to be "over it" for awhile. But I can visit it. I can go there physically, and walk through it and look at it through time-has-passed eyes. I can visit it in my imagination and dreams. And I can "go there" in my writing.

I suggest you take a similar dose of immense Source from the places you have lived and gone. From the people you have met there, and lived with there, loved there, partied with, fought with, saw from a distance and never met. From the buildings and landscapes that occupied them. From their histories and stories—how they were built, these places; who built them; who their heroes and villains are. Take from these places the smells you smelled, the tastes you tasted, the sounds you heard, the things you witnessed, the injuries you endured, the epiphanies you had while you were THERE. The connection between writing and place is vast.

I've summed up enough. No manifesto-y bullet points for this chapter. We've already gone way past where we started.

ASSIGNMENT

All memories degrade. I think I read once that the more you remember something and "use the memory," the more it degrades. Memories over time also become composites — they are enhanced in some way by the emotions that surround it, or by what others tell you has happened even if you don't remember it that way, or by photographs of the moment themselves. In which case it is possible that only people with perfect memories are those who have amnesia.

For this assignment, I want you to recall a memory of something that happened in a house or place you lived. It should be something you haven't thought of in a long time. You can decide whether or not to tell what happened, but let the description of the scene do the heavy lifting of indicating the emotion you want to impart. If what happened there was traumatic, for example, imagine the scene has been hit by a natural disaster. If it was a memory of catching your parents dancing alone, let the furniture blush.

Write the poem in two parts. The first part has bright, vivid details. In the second part of the poem, the memory has degraded. Maybe the dining room chairs are missing their arms, and the curtains have taken themselves down. Maybe someone is talking but you can no longer hear their voice or make out what they are saying. Maybe the sidewalks are crumbling, or the movie theatre sign has been burned.

You see that time is running out before the whole thing disappears. You can only keep one artifact of the scene. What is it?

CHAPTER 11: Benjamin Franklining And The Great And Powerful Is

JUMP-OFF POINT: STARTING FROM YOUR RELATIONSHIP TO GOD/NOT-GOD/THE UNIVERSE

This is the final writing exercise before moving on to the section of the book on editing and polishing. Why? Because I like the number seven. Everyone does.

I saved a big one for the last jump-off-exercise: exploring your relationship to God/Not-God/The Universe. As poets, we have the great honor and pleasure of sinking our sharp metaphor teeth into the meatiest of mysteries. The really BIG questions. The BEYOND BIG questions. We get to not only dig into the great themes of Love, Loss, Death, Birth, Parenthood, Childhood, Media, The Body Politic, Power, Money, Society and its shape-shifting quadruplets Class, Race, Gender and Sexuality. We get to go WAY past that. Our minds contain in them the most powerful telescopes that will ever be invented.

It is a very personal thing—the relationship we have to the IS. Our journey to find and cross and uncross the vast but specific boundary of where we end and the world begins, and then the boundary/unboundary between where the world ends and the what-is-beyond-the-world begins—it is the journey of a lifetime. I mean that literally. We will not know the answers to our questions about the beyond-the-world until we die, or perhaps in the seconds just before—I have heard a rumor those seconds contain eons. Maybe what we are preparing to traffic in is all rumor, all hearsay, all untrustworthy gossip and, for that very reason, totally irresistible and titillating.

Now, drawing from the other lessons we've already absorbed either by reading the previous chapters, psychic osmosis, or foreknowledge, let's agree to ground ourselves and our writing about this big Epic relationship in specific details from our own lives or the lives of others that we are obsessed with; our source cup. Let's agree to free-associate like improvisational jazz musicians. Bring the impending cacophony! Let's agree to follow those threads and ideas and emotions that have the greatest electrical charge, the greatest heat in them for us personally. Let's agree to seek out symmetry or intentional asymmetry. Let's be intentional about forging meaning. Let's apply structure and invent restrictions if we need to. Let's take risks and experiment like mad scientists with our vocabulary and poetic devices. Let's get meta, and seek for the poem and pieces of it to mean many things on many levels. Let's keep in mind that the words and the connected-word-phrases we are writing are creating literal neuropathways in our brains, and have the power to change how we see ourselves and the world. Let's not over-worry the connective tissue as we write, but also be obsessed with the connective tissue we see everywhere, all the synchronicities. Let's prepare not only by taking deep breaths and getting centered, but by disarming ourselves – dropping our guard, our assumptions, our disbelief, our expectations. This will allow us to be vulnerable, and to draw from the wealth of strength and wisdom vulnerability has in store for us, always. Grounded with these skills and tools, let's go get our Epic on.

It feels important to point out to you that the poem I wrote for this exercise did NOT come out in 25 minutes. It brewed for over a year-and-a-half, and I took dozens of mini stabs at getting it out of me. But I loved this idea so much, I did not want to waste it. I wanted it to take as long as it needed to arrive at my pen. Some poems just burst forth whole and complete; some need a lot of time to incubate before they are ready to get cracked open. Let's love our children equally. The origins of this particular poem-idea blossomed long before a year-and-a-half ago, when I wrote down on a napkin: "soul. body. jar. ghost. honey."

The origins may have something to do with my first "out-of-body" experience, which occurred when I was eight (the year I was in Mrs. Patton's class), and which I documented in big loopy kid print in a notebook I have saved in a box labeled, "The Archives."

The origins may also have to do with something that dawned on me in my mid-twenties, as I was struggling to recover from a nervous breakdown that arrived right on schedule, about six months after my fathers' last near-suicide attempt. The nervous breakdown manifested as an asthma attack it took me four weeks to realize I was having. Instead of recognizing that I could not breathe, I thought I was just really really stressed out, full of anxiety, and I intended to just wait it out. By the time I couldn't walk up a flight of stairs without losing my breath, and went to an emergency room, my lung capacity was under 30%. They shot me up with prednisone, lectured me about how close to death I had come, and then sent me home with an oral prescription for prednisone I would have to take for six weeks, in diminishing doses, before being put on a daily routine of inhaled corticosteroids. It would take me two years to get off of the corticosteroids. The doctors had told me I would be on them for the rest of my life. (Oh doctors. Oh ignorant authority. Oh men who explain things to me.)

My healing process was an exercise in what I call Benjamin Franklining. It's a brand-new verb that means using the Self as a primary source for all research, experimentation and discovery. Benjamin Franklin's personal journals and daily diaries were rigorous, detailed, and are a staggering and historically educational read.

I taught myself to breathe again by taking short walks every day, of increasing duration. I documented my progress. Within a month, I could walk a mile. I also read everything could I find on the subject of inflammation in the body, its causes and its cures. It is likely that my prolonged emotional stress had built up so much cortisol in my body, I just broke. Cortisol is the hormone secreted in higher levels during the body's "fight or flight" mode, which was evolutionarily intended for quick bursts of energy for survival. It heightens memory, increases immunity, lowers sensitivity to pain, and helps maintain homeostasis. But if stress is chronic, and high levels of cortisol in the bloodstream are prolonged, the consequences include impaired cognitive performance, suppressed thyroid function, blood sugar imbalances, decreased bone density and muscle tissue, higher blood pressure, lowered immunity, and a slew of other devastating shit.[24]

Taking charge of my own recovery, I quit smoking (not a hard thing to do when you can't breathe oxygen). I changed my diet completely, cutting out all wheat and glutens and processed foods and sugars (though many fruits were allowed and beloved). I invented a yogurt blueberry flax shake I drank every morning. I made vegetable soups and mushroom soups (mushrooms have magical anti-inflammatory properties), found ways to include rosemary, turmeric, and uncooked extra-virgin olive oil whenever and wherever I could. I ate lots of fresh raw vegetables and greens, lots of romaine and spinach and basil, mostly tossed in a dressing I made by blending EVO, rice vinegar, mango, chives, honey and sea salt. (Try that recipe. You're welcome.) (Also, interesting side note: though I did not stop writing during this cleansing and healing, I *did* stop attending poetry events of any kind. I didn't just cut out carbs, people. I cut out the potential for any unintended harm from community.)

In short, for the first time in my life, I resolved to get to know my body and find out what it needed. It needed very particular things nutritionally, especially while recovering from inflammation-caused asthma. It needed lots of movement, from walking to stretching to lifting loads. It needed a predictable circadian rhythm, which included 7-9 hours of sleep every night. It also needed laughter, and conversation, and dancing in my underwear to Prince's Greatest Hits. It needed orgasms (see: dancing naked in my underwear to Prince, et al). It needed me to listen to it when it was sending me signals like hunger, tiredness, pain, tension, and emotion, and to learn how to interpret those signals correctly so that I could self-monitor and give myself what I needed when I needed it. And finally, it needed me to breathe, intentionally, and to stop, often and regularly. (Quick deferential nod to the amazing yoga-instructor-instructor Trinity Capili, who reminds me constantly that even though I'm not a sitter-meditator, or a yogi—unless you count Thai massage where they perform yoga ON you, which feels SO good—that what really matters is breathing. Just breathe.)

All of this got me wondering, why had I neglected my body for so long? What was *that* about? I reflected long and deep. And what emerged for me was a radical thought—I had been taught, from an early age, that I was NOT my body; that I was a "soul." In other words, I was raised in the Christian church. I had never before thought to challenge this basic, underlying assumption. My ethos of suspension of disbelief had made it natural to believe in the soul, or the spark, even as I systematically rejected all organized religious dogma; even as I embraced a belief that when we die, we don't go anywhere, but everywhere. I believe death is quite literally a from dust-to-dust situation as we are returned to the earth, or become ash and smoke. Whatever energy there was in us that fueled our consciousness just dissipates back into the greater energy field, as no energy can be created nor destroyed. We rejoin the mysterious IS.

Where did the "soul" idea come from originally? And how had it shaped me, to believe I was not my body? Yes, my neglect of my body and my health also had something to do with the common death-wishing of terrible youth. The premonition that so many of us have that we will die young, via accident or malice or self-destruction, so, you know, Fuck IT! Fuck the body-as-temple! Fuck everything! Nihilism party and everyone under 25 is invited!

It is so shocking to us at some point to discover that death did not happen. This shock might arrive quietly, softly, on its own, snuck into the icing of a birthday cupcake. Or it might arrive following a real health crisis, or a near-death-experience, in the wake of which we realize suddenly how badly we want to LIVE. "So now what?" we think. Or, "Oh shit." *I have to figure out how to live now, and I don't know how.* Let's give ourselves some deserved compassion by acknowledging the fact that the frontal lobe—responsible for our ability to strategize and plan, to think through and map out choices and consequences, to literally think *ahead*—is the part of the brain that finishes developing *last*, and not until around the mid-twenties. If you are older than that, and you have not gotten smarter and wiser, you *might* be doing something wrong. Look in to it.

But back to our ten-thousand topics. I allowed this new-to-me idea to roam around in my head and rearrange the furniture there—I *was* my body. And "I" was not entirely located in my brain. This thing we call the subconscious, it might *be* my body. These ideas were confirmed, expanded and elucidated by a rapid absorption of popular neuro-science (i.e., nueroscientific research digestible by non-PhDs). The work and books of Candace Pert, in particular, were very helpful, especially her book *Molecules Of Emotion: The Science Behind Mind-Body Medicine.* You should totally go add it to your now-lengthy recommended reading list. Her early work in the study of the causes of HIV had led her to fascinating and fundamental scientific discoveries about neuropeptides, and how they work in the psychoimmunoendicrine network. (I'll pause and give you a minute to untangle that conjugation.) (Ready?) She shorthands this network by just calling it the mindbody. But the information she offers up so readably about how all the information systems in our body and brain are connected, and why that matters in understanding how emotions affect our physical bodies, our immune systems, our memories, our cognitive functioning—epiphany-ville.

So there I am, years later, in a breakfast joint, having just finished some poached eggs and rye toast, and this loose idea for a poem comes out of nowhere: write about how you were taught you were a "soul," write about that idea's evolution. I had vague memories of my child-mind understandings of what "soul" meant, my confusion and fears about ghosts, and grabbed the only clean napkin left on the table and the credit-card-bill-signing-pen and wrote "soul. body. jar. ghost. honey."

You've been so patient, in all these chapters, while I take my sweet goddamned time trying to describe my process to you, as wholly and completely as is possible for me. I am grateful that you are reading this book, that you are getting to know not just how I write, but who I am and where I come from and how I live. I feel like I can trust you with this information. I feel like great things are going to come from it, from my utterly terrifying vulnerability at all moments of writing this book. Here's the poem:

ON BEING RAISED CHRISTIAN AND TAUGHT ENGLISH

When they told me I had a "soul"
I thought they meant I was some kind of bottle;
that something liquid and the color of burning rainbows
had been poured in to me when I was born.
If I stared at the sun with my eyes closed, I could see it.

Then they told me about "ghosts"
and I knew I had been wrong: what they put in me
to make me *me* was not molten, it was white me-shaped air,

the thick wife of breath. I was a balloon filled with smoke.
My body, a thin string tied to it by a knot.

Then they told me ghosts weren't real, just "figments,"
a word I thought meant the way water color paints
disappear into water, getting lighter and lighter,
nothing to soak them in.

The "soul" was not liquid, or air, or solid.
But it *was* a thing. You could lose it.
Some people, they said, were soulless.
Some people had a lot of soul.
Some people sold their souls.

I saw my first manmade beehive the summer I was seven.
I was allowed to go close to the frenzy of bees
by wearing a hat with ghost-fine netting.
The beekeeper reached in to the beecloud
and pulled out chunks of comb dripping with gold.

The beekeeper said every cell of the comb
was either filled with honey or unborn bees.
The bees watched us and did not watch us;
they sang in alarm and sang with worry to make sweetness.

I was also made of "cells."
Was the soul, then, more like honey?
Were some of my cells filled with unborn me's?
Was God the Queen Bee or the worker bees?
Were the stars flowers?

Questions filled me like helium, so many questions.
My mind was a balloon that expanded and floated up
and got lighter the heavier it was and would never pop,
not until it did, not until the thing they called "death,"
the thing that was the place the soul went
when the body stopped breathing.

I had many questions about that, too.
If ghosts weren't real, how did anyone know
what death was like? Where it took you?
If death is a place you go to,
is it the same place that you come from?
Is it the place where the souls are made?

Were the souls made from other souls, like honey from pollen?
Like pollen from flowers? Like flowers from seeds?
Who makes the seeds?

The only questions I didn't ask were these:
why did they want me to believe I was NOT my body in the first place?
If they knew all the things I didn't know yet, why did they look
the way they looked when I asked my questions out loud?
Why did they look so worried?

Some notes on the choices I made in writing this poem at-long-last:

- Faced with such an important narrative, I went in simply, so as not to overwhelm myself, and told it chronologically.

- I grounded this poem with real concrete experiences that were specific and relatable : closing your eyes while staring into the sun; learning about and being afraid of ghosts as a child; getting to see a beehive up close; asking my parents and the adults around me LOTS of questions, and getting corrected, or worse—stunning them into silence.

- I tried to keep my vocabulary relatively simple, to underscore that these are the ideas and questions and epiphanies of a child, who is, at most, seven or eight-years-old.

- I chose objects/imagery that would have been very common in my life back then, also to underscore the child-like tone: bottles, sunshine, balloons, water color paints, helium (yeah!), bees, honey, flowers, seeds.

- And even further to this tone-tight-point, I used the stream of questions in the second-to-last stanza to firmly stay the poem in child-voice.

- I kept as close to the literal ideas I had had as a child, as true to the source material as I could, while leaving room for creative license, as, obviously, I would never have put these thoughts into these words back then.

- I used repetition of imagery to add yummy notes of connection and dings! of synchronicity to the poem. (Um, where did that sentence come from? Am I describing a fine merlot or a poetic process?)

- I ended with the word "worried" to echo back to the only other time I use a form of that word in the poem, the line where the bees "worry to make sweetness." Worry, it turns out, has five distinct meanings in the dictionary, and I mean all of them at once. I will share those with you here, so you don't have to go look them up:

wor•ry

[*wur*-ee, *wuhr*-ee] verb, -ried, -ry•ing, noun, plural -ries.

verb (used without object)
1. to torment oneself with or suffer from disturbing thoughts; fret.
2. to move with effort: an old car worrying uphill.

verb (used with object)
3. to torment with cares, anxieties, etc.; trouble; plague.
4. to seize, especially by the throat, with the teeth and shake or mangle, as one animal does another.
5. to harass by repeated biting, snapping, etc.

- The "mangle" and "harass" definitions of worry *I was not even aware of* until I looked the definition up for you, right now. I was only aware of the word's meanings surrounding anxiety and work. But oh my goddess! How far they go! How deftly they assist me in my attempts at getting my ultimate meaning across: I felt mangled, harassed, broken, hurt by this teaching that I was not my body. This teaching, with all its good and holy and perfectly natural intentions had had serious consequences, and damaged me in ways that, thank "God," were not irreparable.

- I went meta! In so many places. I'll let you interpret as you will.

- I played with the connective tissue of the universe, literally and figuratively, to underscore the thesis I was playing with about what it is that makes us *us*, and connects us with everything else.

SUMMARY:

- Traffic in more than facts; traffic in rumors. Traffic in what exists and does not exist. Traffic in everything. And in Everything. It's your right and your privilege as a poet.

- Sometimes poems take a long, long time to write. Don't sweat it. Be patient with them. They are important, and deserve your forbearance, perseverance, restraint, and submission.

- Your physical health, your homeostasis, is VERY IMPORTANT. If you do not take care of your body, it will affect more than just your immune system and health; it will have a dramatic effect on you emotionally and mentally, and it might make you crazy, or turn you in to an asshole who is grouchy and dark all the time and takes it out on everyone else. Or worse, and I don't want to go there. You need very specific nutrients to function cognitively and at full creative capacity. Please take the time to read up on nutrients and how to get them into your body at the nonprofit World's Healthiest Foods website: www.whfoods.org. You also need to eat *regularly* (keep that blood sugar from crashing!), sleep enough, move enough, breathe intentionally, have conversations with friends and strangers, and experience dumb joy as often as possible.

- Self-maintenance is about checking in with yourself often and openly, and listening to the signals your body is giving you so clearly about what you need. Please attend to your needs. Attend to them *before* you attend to those of others, if at all possible. There are limits to what your body can take, and you don't want to meet them.

- Challenge your basic assumptions about yourself, about your life, about the meaning of life, about the world, about others, about the IS. Try to figure out where they came from. Untie those inner knots so you can turn them into pretty, flowy braids; so you can weave together healthier, saner beliefs and ideas, beliefs that make you happy, beliefs that make you want to LIVE. ALL CAPS!

- Use your word choices, your imagery, your juxtapositions, your repetitions, all of it, to create the tone and voice that you mean for your poem to have. That **tone** is everything. I bolded that word for a reason. Controlling your poem's tone is the only pseudo-control you have over how total strangers will read your work. More on that later.

- Get out those dictionaries and thesauri! Or bookmark the online versions on your web browser! You are never more than a minute away from the word you are looking for.

- You can always learn more from the dictionary. As a writer, it is your bible. It is your holy sacred tomb. Study it forever.

- Making connections between abstract ideas that force epiphanies in yourself and others about how things really *are* connected should be a central mission of your work as a writer and a thinker and a human being, you know, that thing that started from stardust and is now causing all this beauty and destruction and chaos and love and babies.

- Be brave. Risk asking big, unanswerable questions.

- (Deep breath before this one. This last one I mean with every fiber of my being.) Confront your fear of death. We are all going to die. None of us knows when; our lifespan is unpredictable. What is predictable: until we do die, we are going to know and love many many people who die. It is going to break our hearts over and over and over. There will be times when the pain of this grief and loss feels unbearable. It is not. Bear it. *Be* a bear. According to some shamans I chatted with once at a Renaissance Faire, the Bear as a power animal is a symbol of strength, introspection, knowledge, dreams and transformation. Be *that*. Teach others how to be it. Our time is precious. Do something amazing with yours. Have beautiful dreams. Manifest some of them. Be kind to yourself and be compassionate to others. Follow your happiness and follow your fear, which is sometimes ecstatic joy in disguise. Whatever you do with your time here, don't waste it. Waste your glitter instead. Throw it on everything and everyone. There will always be more where that came from.

ASSIGNMENT

You've never been told anything about how the universe began. You've never heard of a "God" or "Gods" or heard of anything called the Big Bang Theory. But you know what? You've never thought about it that much. You are playing a board game with a little kid who you are just crazy about, and just as the kid is about to take a turn, he or she turns to ask you: "Where did the sky come from?" You want to tell the truth, but you don't know it. Answer the question.

CHAPTER 12:
More Fresh, Cold Prompts from the Prompt Snow-Machine in Mindy's Brain to Melt and Smelt into Hot Burning Poems

After reading the seven exercises on jumping off of poem cliffs and absorbing some knowledge about process possibilities, you may have the powerful desire to go straight to your medium of choice and fire off some more poetry. So, just in time for chapter 12, here are twelve prompts for you to use or not use, to change or rearrange, to subvert or convert, for the creation of new writing.

Prompt #1: Imagine your ideal creative office space. Restrictions:

- It must be located on another planet or celestial object.

- It cannot be in the shape of a square or rectangle.

- It has to have doors and windows, and they cannot be made of expected materials like wood or glass.

- It must have a ceiling and a floor, even if they are inversions of those concepts. You must describe the ceiling and the floor, or the not-ceiling/not-floor.

- It must have tools in it, tools that do not exist on Earth. Tell us what they are.

- There is an animal that lives there. What is it? How does it behave?

- You must have routines you perform upon entering and exiting the space. What are they?

- There is a sign on the entrance/exit. What does the sign say? (Is this the title of the piece?)

Prompt #2: You are staying the night at the house of a stranger, but who is a friend-of-a-friend-of-a-friend. You slept in an unfamiliar room, in an unfamiliar bed. You have a dream about that stranger, about the house, about the room, a dream that is deeply dream-logic-bizarre but explains everything about who this stranger is. The dream is so vivid, you have trouble upon waking deciding whether it was real or not. What was the dream?

Prompt #3: A shaman walks into a bar and tells a joke to the bartender, and the when the bartender laughs he or she is suddenly transformed into something or someone else entirely. Describe the shaman. Describe the bartender. Tell the joke. Tell us what happens to the bartender.

Prompt #4: You are at the annual meeting of the Gods and Goddesses of Weather. You are assigned a particular weather pattern or weather event to be in charge of for the following weather-work-year. What is your assignment? How do you execute it? Do you fail? Succeed? Something else? How does executing it change you, magical-realism-style, by imparting you with one of that weather pattern's qualities, powers or gifts?

Prompt #5: Think back. Tell us what you remember about your first day of kindergarten, and through that, what you were like when you were five-years-old. Tell it from the perspective of the objects in the classroom, who are meeting five-year-old-you for the first time.

Prompt #6: Cleaning out your closet, you find a box of old New Year's Resolutions. You barely remember writing them, some of them are so old. You have a healthy, self-deprecating laugh at your old ambitions. One of these resolutions you accomplished. One of them you did not. Write a poem in three parts:

1. Finding the old resolutions
2. What you failed to follow through on
3. The change you committed to and made

Please, if you would, sprinkle the poem with imagery and vocabulary that suggest a New Year's party (Chinese or Western calendar New Year, or, shoot, even Mayan if you're familiar.). Reminder: some New Year's parties are real bummers. Some are the best parties ever. The objects and people and music at those parties can be described in a way as to connote the mood or tone of the party and, thus, the message(s) of your poem.

Prompt #7: You discover you are the center, the crux, the crucial mechanism in some massive, Rube-Goldberg-ian machine scheme plot to destroy the world. You have been paranoid about this for some time. There have been signs, ominous warnings. How is it revealed to you, this plan They have for you? Who are They? Maybe you don't know! Maybe you do know. Maybe you will tell us. Maybe you won't, for fear of being assassinated. However you found it, you found out just in the nick of time. You have a choice to make about whether or not to allow yourself to be triggered. What do you do?

Prompt #8: There is a car parked outside of your house or apartment. You can see from your window it is an older, silver, sedan-ish car, but even from this distance you can see it has been meticulously maintained. The driver's side door is wide open, the headlights are on, and no one is in the car, so you go outside to investigate. The car is clean inside and out and is empty except for the following things: the keys in the ignition; a full gas tank; a hastily written note on the passenger seat that says only, "Dear New Owner, I don't have time to explain, but—" and then nothing further; and three items in the unlocked glove box—an owner's manual for a 2000 Infinity g20, title transfer documents with the names left blank, and a map. You do not over think it! You act! You get in the driver's seat, close the door, and turn the keys in the ignition. What happens?

Prompt #9: Standing in line at the grocery store, you cannot help but overhear an intense whispered argument between the couple in front of you in line. A strange, déjà-vu-ish feeling comes over you. You have seen this same argument before, but between two different people, under completely different circumstances. Set up the scene if you want, or don't. Alternate between the dialogue of the arguing couple at the grocery store and the remembered argument, indicating their difference by using italics for the past, remembered one. Consider weaving in a parenthesized third argument, one you are having with yourself, in your own head, about a significant, urgent, imminent choice that needs to be made in your life. You are unsure about which course to take, your pros-and-cons-ing it, and opposed aspects of your personality are fighting for rank.

Prompt #10: You meet a person who cannot see, hear, or speak. You discover another way to communicate. What is it? What do you try to tell this person? What do they try to tell you? How?

Prompt #11: There is a sound coming from somewhere in the room you are in. It does not belong there. What is it? How do you recognize it, and that it doesn't belong? How did it get there? How can you free it?

Prompt #12: Pick one of the following: your mother, your father, a sibling, or someone in your life who fits one of those bills and represents that relationship to you. Write a persona poem in this person's perspective. You may choose to write this poem in two parts, or as two companion poems. In one, you try to get as close as is possible to writing in their voice, from the perspectives they actually has, about the things they actually care about. In the second, you go pure wish-fulfillment: you write in their voice but about what you wish they cared about, how you wish they saw things/someone/you.

BONUS PROMPT!!! [mad, drunken cheering]

Lucky Prompt #13: Choose a celebrity, dead or alive. (Here's winking at you, Brad Liening.) It could be a famous scientist, an iconoclast from another time or from this time, a spiritual or political leader; it could be a famed actor or actress, a painter, a sculptor, a dancer, a writer. But it must be someone firmly lauded in the collective consciousness of pop-culture or history, either because they were/are beloved, or because they were/are a pariah. Have a free form conversation with this person. Use details you have researched about their personal lives, details they either shared freely in interviews (and which should therefore be viewed as from a suspect narrator) or details others revealed or dug up about them that were probably a HUGE violation of their human right to privacy. Use details from their body of work. Stalk this person on the internet and elsewhere until you are satisfied you have a strong, vivid impression of their true nature, or at least of their public mask. How did the opportunity for this conversation come about? Ask them what you want to know. What is their physical response to the questions you ask? Do they answer your questions? What do they say? What does that mean about them? What does that mean about you? What does that mean about all of us, about society, about our fame obsessed, celebrity saturated media culture? What does that mean about what it's like to be human, living as an object and a subject at the same time? What does that mean about our fear of death, or not being remembered after we are gone? Go for the JUGULAR on this one. Eat this prompt alive. Chew through that meat till you get to the bone.

ON EDITING POETRY

*"I wanted to change the world. But I have found
that the only thing one can be sure of changing is oneself."*
—*Aldous Huxley*

"Even the best epiphany still needs to be edited."
—*Jonah Lehrer*

CHAPTER 13: Paper Snow Flaking 101

Remember when you were a kid (or very recently)—you had to make paper snowflakes for winter decorations? You were taught to take a square piece of paper, fold it in half diagonally so that it was a winged triangle, then fold it similarly again and again until it was a small fat triangle, but not too thick to cut through. You were told to clip shapes into the triangle's edges—mostly other triangles with two short snips, but any shape would do. Then you unfolded it and…voila! Not what you thought it would look like AT ALL! So you got another square and tried again, learning from your last cuts, and again, learning from those, until you saw that you could make it look very different every time. With each attempt, you got closer and closer to making it look like what you wanted it to look like.

You were also probably told at some point that each snowflake—real snowflakes, not paper ones—was unique. Have you ever had the chance to look at a big fat snowflake up close? One that caught, perhaps, on your mitten, and froze there for a moment in its original form, before melting away to damp nothing? Were you in awe? Were you dumbstruck by the grace of that perfect icy mandala, its tiny symmetrical network of branches radiating out from a center? How delicate! How intricate! How temporary, this passing moment of pure natural art!

Meteorologists are a bit divided on the uniqueness question, saying prudent, science-y things like Hans Verlinde does, when he begins, "It depends on how we define snowflake."[25] Doesn't everything, Hans, depend on how we define our words, whether or not we share their meaning? He goes on, "Let's be specific." Yes, Hans, let's. "[Let's] define a snowflake as a single, vapor-grown ice crystal. I would say with great confidence that all crystals are different on a molecular level, purely because there are differences in the atomic structure of the atoms making up the water molecule, and hence, in the water molecules themselves." However, despite this provable atomic difference, two snowflakes can look identical, even under a microscope.

Many factors influence the shape and structure of real snowflakes: temperature, vapor concentrations, dirt or dust in the air, whether children are watching. "We cannot know for certain that every snowflake is unique, simply because we cannot observe them all." Well, yes Hans, that's obviously true. And this discussion of snowflakes could go on and on because they are created in cirrus clouds, and they change the clouds as they are formed in them, and cirrus clouds play a large role in what Hans calls "the earth's energy budget, and hence climate." It's all connected, man. It's all intricate. It's *all* delicate.

But we are not; I am scientifically certain of this, cirrus clouds. We are poets. We cannot replicate real snowflakes as the cirrus clouds do without crazy expensive lab equipment and funding from the federal government. But we can turn plain old paper into something equally breathtaking. We can apply our vast skills of mental origami. We can use the scissors of our sharp self-critique. We can learn from every attempt, every word choice, every cut. We can experiment with making something turn out the way we mean it to. Am I getting a little heavy-handed with my snowflake metaphors? YES! I am bringing out the metaphor hammers! I am hitting you on the head, softly and snow-flakily with a flurry of metaphors! Welcome to section of the book on editing.

The previous section of this book was designed to seduce you in to writing, get you addicted to experimenting with your creative process, and push you in the direction of writing about what has emotional charge and meaning for you personally. It was a big subjectivity marathon. And getting more subjective about the subject was the subject. Poetry that could not have been written by anyone else is the kind of poetry I love, and I am totally indoctrinating you! But hopefully I am indoctrinating you in YOU. If you have been writing from some of the prompts in this book, it has been a total YOU-fest. I imagine it spurred all kinds of things I cannot imagine.

Editing is an opposite exercise; it is an exercise in objectivity. We have to get out of our minds, our writer-minds, and attempt to see the poems from a critical, outside perspective. Gaining this objectivity can be as simple as walking away from the poems for awhile, letting them rest, letting them take your credit cards and go backpacking in Europe. When you see them again, they will be strangers to you. You may have brand new insight about whether they work, and how they work, and then whether and how they could work better. But it is usually not that simple.

Honing your editing skills is crucial to becoming a better writer. Still, many of us avoid editing like it's a collection agent, or some other incarnation of "the man." We prefer the part where we just get to write, and don't have to think about what anyone else will think, because being an artist means having truly original thoughts, and just "being," and who cares what anyone else thinks anyway? And you know what? Fair enough! If you love the work, crown it done. (Fun note: I can count on one hand the number of times a poems has just, you know, *arrived*, and I thought it was perfect. And every single one of them eventually got edited.)

Others of us worry we will ruin our writing by over-thinking it. This is not a completely paranoid thought. The fantastic Billy Collins poem comes to mind called "Introduction to Poetry." In it he describes his attempts to teach his students to enter poems poetically, asking them to "walk inside the poem's room/ and feel the walls for a light switch." But in the end, "all they want to do/ is tie the poem to a chair with rope/ and torture a confession out of it./ They begin beating it with a hose/ to find out what it really means." It's not a poem about editing your work. It's a poem about reading other people's work like bulls shop for china. But since we're attempting to be objective about our work, I feel it applies. We should have some reservations about editing our poems to death. Our intention is to edit them to life.

And maybe all of that is deflection and defense. Maybe we avoid editing because we are just afraid of what we will discover about our darlings when we do it with total sincerity. Just as we need to be braver in what we write poems about, we need to steel ourselves for the difficult task of editing.

I have broken up the discussion on editing into five interlocking parts: 1) the tools you have at your disposal and should use for editing, 2) advice on editing for content, 3) advice on editing for context, 4) advice on editing for language/rhythm/musicality, and 5) advice on editing for form. Before we dive in, let's take a few shots of courage in the formguise of quotes from great thinkers and writers, quotes that scare me with their intelligence, their rightness, and their implications about the task ahead. Let's let this be our editing invocation:

"Poetry proposes that the language you are using to render experience helps shape the experience; that language is crucial to the act of creating your life." –Rob Breszny

"Words have no power to impress the mind without the horror of their reality."—Edgar Allen Poe

"If language is not correct, then what is said is not what is meant; if what is said is not what is meant, then what must be done remains undone; if this remains undone, morals and art will deteriorate; if justice goes astray, the people will stand about in helpless confusion. Hence there must be no arbitrariness in what is said. This matters above everything."—Confucius

"You're wrong if you think your manuscript isn't surrounded by a hazy invisible cloud of context and possibility."—Chuck Wendig

"We are clouds, and terrible things happen/ in clouds." –Dean Young

Thank you, Chuck, and thank you Dean, for helping me bring this baby back around to clouds. It is true what you wrote, Dean. But much more then terrible things happen in clouds. Snowflakes happen. Rainbows happen (rainbows that are discs!!! Oh holy everything!). And I'm certain, when the light is right, a fair amount of glittering.

CHAPTER 14:
Your Editing Tools: a Field Guide

The very first thing I do when I want to edit a poem is I read it out loud. If at all possible, I also first put it in to a format other than the one it was initially written in: if it's a poem of mine written messily by hand, I rewrite it on fresh paper; if it was typed into a computer, I print it out. The act itself of turning the poem into a new object helps you get some much-needed objectivity. I then read it out loud, slowly and repeatedly, and make notes.

I want to suggest that your primary tools for editing (besides, of course, a pen or pencil or trained squid) are your voice and your ear. So before we really get into this, I think we need to ground ourselves in a primer on how the ear works, on how sound works. My apologies to those among you who are science-averse and are sighing heavily, like *MORE science? In a book on poetry? I thought I was here to be filled with the gold spirit yolk of metaphor, not squaresville science jargon?* But also, get on board already. I have my reasons and they are good ones. (And again, if you're not interested in how things work and are connected, what are you doing reading a book on writing poetry?)

ON SOUND, THE EAR, AND THE BRAIN

The Basics:

Sound (in air) is made when air molecules vibrate and move away from the vibrating source in a pattern called waves, which we call, well, sound waves. Sound is a mechanical, longitudinal wave that moves in all directions and travels in waves of compressions and rarefactions (expansions) as it passes through mediums. A sound wave drawn on paper by scientists for study is almost always on an XY-axis graph, and looks like this:

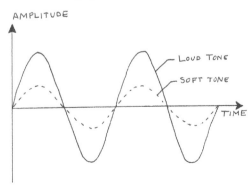

The strength of the waves are called Sound Pressure Levels, or SPLs (Science loves acronyms. They help it move at faster speeds.). These "SPLs" are measured in decibels. The slower and more widespread the wave is, the deeper the sound. (And the farther it can travel—hence all that base-bomping out of tricked-out Corollas.) The faster/higher/tighter the wave, the higher the sound. A healthy ear can perceive frequencies from 20 Hz to 20,000 Hz. The frequencies between 500Hz and 4000 Hz are the happy medium where speech from the human voice lives.

Sound waves are first collected in the outer ear, referred to as the auricle (or Pinna, but I like auricle better, for its homonym value.). The waves then travel through the ear canal (the thing we stick Q-tips in against the advice of our doctors), and meet up with the ear drum, which is called a drum for a reason, because when a sound wave strikes it, it vibrates. These vibrations then travel through the three smallest bones in your body: the malleus, stapes and incus, more commonly (and descriptively) known as the hammer, stirrup and anvil.

Now we enter the cochlea! All hail the cochlea! And June Melby's song-poem about the cochlea! (We are actually entering the inner ear as a whole, which also houses the vestibular system which is responsible for balance, but we're here to hear, not walk.) The cochlea is spiral-shaped and looks like an alien seashell and is, in fact, named from the Greek word for snail shell. It has a magical fluid in it, and is lined with specialized fine hair cells. At the opening of the cochlea is a connective membrane called the oval window (which I try to picture as a cellophane-y, flattened two-dimensional fish-bowl version of the Oval Office.). That membrane transforms the mechanical motion into a hydraulic pressure wave in the fluid. This wave movement bends the hair cells into dancing, and this dancing is what creates the impulses in the vestibular nerves. I know this is *sounding* very complicated already, but I promise, I am high-wiring the edge of over-simplification.

The hearing mechanism consists of two units you are very familiar with: the left ear and the right ear. (Hi guys!) The medulla oblongata (the lower half of the brain stem) receives the signals from the vestibular nerves in both ears at differing timings and strengths, depending on where the sound is coming from, how the head is turned, and the distance of the sound. This difference in timing and intensity is what creates the three-dimensional aspect that sound has.

The Not-So-Basics:

The mighty and primitive brain stem then sends the signals to the midbrain, which passes them on to the auditory cortex of the temporal lobes. It is the neurons in the auditory cortex that signal-baton it all to the rest of the nervous system and spinal cord.

Interesting to note: only a small minority of available auditory nerves respond with any verve at all (I had to, with the internal rhyming, I *had* to) when exposed to any particular sound—really only about 5% have what would be considered a "high firing rate." Studies conducted by Anthony Zador, PhD at the CSHL Swartz Center for Computational Neuroscience, have focused on exploring and explaining why we are able to pay selective attention to things.[26] Why we can hear, for example, our friend complain lightly about her new horrible boss at work while being surrounded by a cacophony of traffic, or loud music, or other voices. What they have discovered is that each neuron may have an optimal stimulus to which it is particularly sensitive; there may be specialized nerves for "best friend's voice" or "phone ringing" or "Phil Collins." Zador posits, "Your entire sensory apparatus is there to make successful representations of the outside world. Sparse representations may make sensory stimuli easier to recognize or remember…The goal of sensory processing is to take a signal, like a sound or a vision, and use it to drive behavior." Like sway-sobbing in front of a jukebox to "Against All Odds (Take a Look at Me Now)."

So what happens next? Well, a lot of things. It depends. Thankfully, many scientists have devoted their careers to watching brains listen to music, which I am going to equate with poetry, and their discoveries offer some answers. (Remember back when I recommended *This Is Your Brain On Music* by Daniel J. Levitin? SUCH a thriller.) The area of the brain responsible for first integrating intensity and pitch information relayed from the cochlea is the trusty old brain stem because this initial information was and is important for the basic survival of our species. The brain stem is at-the-ready to prompt immediate physical responses after, say, locating tigers, or an oncoming speeding car, or a potential mate. "This 'crude' information," as researcher Feyza Sancar puts it, "is then sent to areas of the cerebral cortex, like the auditory cortex, for achieving complex assessment.[27] She goes on to explain something pertinent:

> In particular, the auditory cortex interprets sounds within the context of what has preceded… The right-brain auditory cortex specializes in determining hierarchies of harmonic relations and rich overtones whereas the left auditory hemisphere deciphers relationships between successions of sounds (i.e.-- the sequencing of sounds and perception of rhythm). It should be noted that the right-brain auditory cortex is particularly adept at analyzing the highly harmonic vowel sounds of language… [and] the left brain is involved in the sequencing of words and ideas and is considered the 'seat' of language. In fact, through MRI scans, it has been recognized that one of the areas of the brain used to decipher language may also 'contain' the ability to conceive

absolute pitch…From this information, it can be inferred that music and language may be interpreted and deciphered in similar ways as well as by similar brain structures.

I knew it! Now, in order to really process melody or poetry, many "higher" functioning areas of the brain are involved, like our old-mid-twenties-developing-friends the frontal lobes, and those areas of the brain responsible for long and short-term memory and learning processes. (If I veered off into a discussion of how memory and learning works…well, I won't. But if you have the inclination to familiarize yourself with the current research on that, I think it would make for a titillating Saturday afternoon. If you're a knowledge whore like me.) This is where we arrive at the hippocampus and, possibly, the whole point of this primer. Back to you Ms. Sancar:

> It has been observed that animals exposed to Mozart…completed spatial mazes faster and with fewer errors. From these observations, it is has been theorized that music [/poetry] and spatial temporal reasoning may activate the same neural pathways in the hippocampus of the brain. It could be argued that listening to and interpreting music [/poetry] with complex patterns activate the neuronal pathways in the hippocampus, which can lead to an increased efficacy of the neurons. The increase in the efficacy of neurons may in turn encourage the formation of new synaptic connections. This touches upon the idea of physical contiguity, where signals can get from one place to another only if there are synaptic connections between the two areas. In terms of this principal, it has been proposed that musicians [and poets] (who both extensively listen [to] and perform music [and poetry]) may possess a larger number of biochemical links or pathways between and within structures in the brain that are common to everybody.

Do you see what I am getting at with this whole "let's talk about how the brain works" thing? Writing poetry, reading it out loud, editing it, re-writing it, reading it out loud again—it is making you smarter. It is making your brain fancier. This whole process of reading out loud and listening is making you a better writer. More pathways, more electrical impulses pulsing, more glitter. Here endeth the lesson.[28]

* * *

So you've got your voice. You've got your ear. And your ear is connected very wonderfully to everything your brain has ever stored, even the stuff you cannot easily recall—it's in there somewhere, in the amaze maze. This includes, significantly, everything you have ever read—poems, novels, news articles, Oprah's facial expressions. By listening to the words you wrote by speaking them out loud, you will know when something doesn't sound right. You will know where to begin and head with the edits.

Some obvious indicators that editing is needed:

- **As you read it out loud, some phrases got stuck in your mouth and**

came out awkwardly and clumsily. Those are problem phrases. There is something wrong with the word choices, or their arrangement, if they didn't flow out easily. Rearrange it. Rewrite it. Or cut it entirely.

- **You lost your breath while reading a line or stanza.** Perhaps there is just too much going on in it. Or perhaps your punctuation and/or line breaks did not allow for proper pauses and breaths. Fix it.

- **You lost the thread of the thought or idea while reading it.** I mean, even you didn't understand where you came from and where you were going with it, or what you meant exactly in that part of the piece. This could indicate several things. There could simply be connective tissue missing that you need to write and work in. Or maybe you didn't have a clear intention with the line or section of the piece, and hence it came out unclear. But if it's not making real sense, not in the context of the ultimate intention of the poem, it doesn't belong in the poem. Maybe it belongs in another poem. Keep it. Put it somewhere, this and other "orphan lines." As poet Tony Brown says with great understanding and compassion (and you'll hear *way* more about Tony in a minute), "It's tough when you realize that the line that you were in love with, the one that got the whole ball of wax rolling, now no longer fits with the poem in front of you. Which is why I keep a folder of 'orphan lines' on the desktop for just such occasions. It's pretty full."

- **A word sounded jarring and out of place to you.** This means that all your word choices are not singing the same sound song. I am not saying that you should apply onomatopoeia often and liberally (or am I?), but as you no doubt absorbed from early and possibly horrible phonics lessons (do they still teach reading with phonics?), letters, letter combinations and their masters, words, have very different sounds. Some words have hard sounds, like "clunk" or "whack" or "guilt." Even more words have soft sounds, like "fluidity" or, ironically, "melamine," or "cinders," or the wildly popular word combination "cellar door." When word combinations have complementary sounds, it is very pleasing to the ear aesthetically and is called "euphony." There is a whole field called phonaesthetics that just studies the euphony and cacophony of words without regard for semantics. Listen as you read for jarring sounds, out of place word-choices causing cacophony, which interrupts the readers ability to lose themselves in the music of your poetry. Change it.

- **You feel confused, emotionally, reading it.** If even you don't know what you're supposed to be feeling; if you're not getting clear, resonating signals from the words; if they are not conducting your emotions like maestros at golden podiums, something isn't working. This is either a content or context issue, which I will discuss more in the following chapters.

- **You heard so many varying images, "parent images," and guiding metaphors, you couldn't easily track them while reading the poem.** Consider that your poem might breathe a sweet sigh of relief if you took some of that weight off. What I refer to as a "parent image" is a sort of master category for a set of similar images, like, for example, water, and it "parents" or guides the appearance of other imagery in the poem, making it watery; lakes appear, or tears, or buoys, or boats, or rain showers. Or shadow imagery to the parent appears, anti-water imagery like oil slicks, or dams, or deserts. Maybe there should only be one "parent image," or two, or five. But the more you have, the more complex it will be for the reader to track, and to extract meaning from their selection. Which ones does the poem need to work, on the level of getting your meaning across? How can you simplify and edit out images that don't harmonize with the master metaphors you are working? Less is more; general, but bendy rule of thumb.

- **Finally, the poem is just long.** Like, really long. You got tired reading it out loud. Is it an epic you are writing? Should it be divided up somehow? Is it really two poems, or three poems, and not one coherent poem?

This is the first phase of editing. (And by that, I mean the phase that comes *after* the pre-first-phase of proof-reading and copy-editing. I am not going to waste anyone's time addressing typos and grammar choices. You have spellcheck, dictionaries, eyeballs and William Strunk Jr. and E.B. White's *The Elements of Style* for all that.) You read the poem out load, you notice and take notes of what does not sound right, and you get to work on fixing it, on rewriting, on rewording, on re-sequencing.

Your goal is that the poem itself can be read aloud in the same, easy way you might have a conversation with a close friend, someone who really "gets you," and who also speaks English (if that is the language you are indeed writing in). That conversation should flow. And if while talking to said friend—possibly a real friend, possibly an imaginary friend, and possibly you just playing the role of the friend, classic-Gestalt-style—they got that squinty scrunchy look on their face, the look that means they do NOT understand what you are saying, you would stop. You would think, *this isn't coming out right.* And you would search yourself for the words that mean what you *mean*. And then you would say them. And then your friend's face would relax and they would say, "Oh, yeah. Totally."

ASSIGNMENT

When you have hit the wall on your ability to be objective, or when you're feeling stuck about a piece—you know some of it doesn't quite work, but you have no idea why—you need to get some outside perspective. Here are some things you could try:

1. Have three people read it out loud to you. You might be surprised by what you hear when it comes out in someone else's voice.

2. Attend a writing workshop (or convince some of your writer friends to start one in your living room). Be fearless about listening to notes on your work. Know that you can ignore all of it in the end, and do what you want. Know that much of what other people say is waaaay more about them than it is about the poem. Know that some people have great insight, but are unpracticed at giving criticism. Or just delight in being contrarians. (There are other, meaner words I could have used for "contrarian," and you know what they are.) Knowing all of this, listen with rapt attention anyway. You will likely have a few things pointed out to you that you did not see about that poem. You may hear someone interpret your poem in a radically different light. You will get actual objective feedback, and your response to it, positive or negative, will help you know what *you* think.

3. Now take the poem out on a date to a local open mic. There is a great deal to be gained from reading your work to an audience. You can get instant emotional feedback from an audience that is listening. Do they laugh at the right parts (or the wrong parts)? Do they sigh or mmmmm? Are they understanding you, tracking the poem from start to finish? Do you feel energy coming from them while you're reading it? If you have the kind of crippling stage fright that extends to being unable to tell a waiter your order is wrong, then this step is too soon for you. BUT! You should do it anyway! You know how to get rid of stage fright? Sheer volume of practice. And if you have never gone to an open mic before, please direct your attention to next chapter.

CHAPTER 15: THE FEEDBACK LOOP

This is a book on writing poems, not on performing poems. But we poets have an incredible leg up on novelists (the whole they-could-make-real-money-thing notwithstanding). That leg up is poetry readings. Our work is short enough that we can share it on a regular basis, and hear other people's work, and be a part of a community of poets that inspire us and impress us and keep us going. And since I've just assigned you to use the open mic as a potential tool for feedback, I thought I would take it a small step further and let you in on what I have absorbed after 20 years of going to poetry readings.

That's somewhere over 4,000 poetry readings. Maybe there was anywhere from 20 to 40 poems per show, and I don't want to do the math, but it's fair to say I have listened to, like, a lot of poetry. Some of that poetry has been impactful and transformative. Some of it has been so funny and creative it made me weep invisible writer tears of jealousy. But the vast majority of it has been bad. Some of that most has been so bad, I wanted to bolt for the coffee shop door because it was killing the thing I love most.

I put the word "feedback" in the title of this chapter because of its multiple meanings. The denotation I am calling upon now is the acoustic one, the "feedback" that means when electrical oscillations between a mic and a PA cause loud screeching murder owl sounds. We've all heard that shriek of feedback. It makes you cringe and cover your ears. And if you go to enough poetry readings, and start to get a taste for the good stuff, you know the cringe in your heart and the shriek in your soul when the bad happens. And for people who are not poets, and do not care for it or know much about it, going to just one poetry reading with their English Major girlfriends and having this experience will make them avoid poetry readings forever.

But screw that hater, and let's forget for a moment that bad performances kill the spread of poetry love. Let's focus on how "the how" of your performance affects you and your journey to becoming a better writer. Reading your poems poorly will make your audience shut down. They may not cover their ears or bolt for the door or start heckling you (unless you are at the Green Mill in Chicago, fair warning), but you will not get what you want out of the experience. What you want is the good feedback loop, when the audience is listening, and you can feel their attention. In this loop, there are moments of resonance and moments when you lose them and you will feel it, and it will tell you what works in your work.

I want you to get this feedback if you want it. So let's discuss three kinds of performance styles that we should all avoid.

#1: Poetry Voice

Haaave *you* eveeerrr, hearrrd a poooet, reeead their pooems in a STILted AWKward waaaay? Over-emphasizing syllables, elongating their vowels, forcing a rhythm, and in general reading the poem with extreme affectation, to add dramatic effect? This particular style of reading a poem is what we call "Poet Voice." If you're unsure what I'm talking about, go rent *So I Married An Axe Murderer*. Mike Myers' send up of performance poets is hilarious. Myers is exaggerating for comic effect, but I have seen this so many times in real life, I'm not sure it *is* an exaggeration. This kind of performance can ruin the most gorgeous piece. Poetry Voice may have its roots in the Beat movement, when poetry and jazz were often performed together. Maybe poets are trying to a-capella that jazz into their poems with just their voices. Please don't do this. Unless you are Bobby McFerrin, or actually have a horn section living in your vocal chords, or are performing a poem about jazz or music that requires this and you are a gifted vocalist, in which case, *yes*.

#2: The Bored Professor

This style is the opposite of the sort of exaggerated performance I just described. It involves reading your poems in a monotonous, flat tone and maybe even with a hint of arrogance. It is more effective than Ambien. (No studies have been done by the FDA, but I'm pretty sure about this.) This is another performance style guaranteed to disengage an audience. I've named it "The Bored Professor" in honor of the many times I've gone out of my way to see a well-known poet whose work I have admired deeply on the page, and seen them read their work in a style that says, "I'd-rather-be-finishing-my-taxes." The worst part is not that I then spend the next hour trying not to fall asleep. The worst part is that, from then on, I hear their bored voices when I read their work and it erases the vivid, haunting beauty it used to have for me. Finally....

#3: Dramatic Burn

This style emerges, I imagine, from exposure to poetry slam and spoken word, and I know I have been guilty of it. It is an over-dramatic performance of a poem because you want your audience to FEEL something, and you think you can accomplish this with a performance orgasm on stage. If the poem has the goods, all it needs is an honest performance that honors it; it can be subtle or it can be fierce, but it should not be forced.

One indicator of Dramatic Burn is the forced-cry. Now, I have actually cried while reading a poem on stage before. It is awful. The first thing that happens is your voice catches and you can't speak. You have triggered the powerful, real emotion in yourself that you were writing from, and it swells up in your throat, and you fight it. You have to push it back down in order to finish reading the poem, or start crying in front of a bunch of strangers, and there is a terrifying vulnerability in this moment. I have felt it enough and seen it enough to know when it is real. When it's real, it is incredibly moving. If it is an act, the audience will know.

Another indicator of Dramatic Burn is when a poet reads the lines so quickly and with so much urgency that the audience misses at least half of them. This is either the poet trying to force momentum for dramatic effect, or salute a sort of punk rock aesthetic, or just an unfortunate side-effect of poetry slam time limits. (In traditional poetry slam competitions, there is a 3-minute time limit imposed on competitors. Poets sometimes have five minutes of awesome they are trying to squeeze into 3 minutes to prevent over-time penalties.) If the audience cannot absorb what you are saying, you will never get that sweet resonance you are looking for. So, my quick and dirty performance tips for reading your poems well on a stage with a microphone:

- Relax! Maybe don't picture the audience naked, but also don't picture them as hostile predators. It's just a poetry reading.

- Adjust the mic once to get it at the right position and then stop messing with it.

- Do some quick banter just to test the mic's hotness, like a "hey there, happy Wednesday everybody." This will give you an idea of how far to stand back from or get close to the mic, depending on your natural vocal range of projection.

- Do not explain the poem before your read it unless there is an absolutely crucial piece of context the whole poem hangs around and, if there is, for the love of all that is holy, keep it brief.

- Do not say, "I just wrote this, and it's not any good or finished, but here we go." Or anything else that lets people know they are about to hear a poem even you don't like. Own your poem.

- Ground yourself for a moment and take a breath.

- Unless the poem calls for a funny or creative delivery, read the poem in your natural conversational voice. It can and should have emotion in it, if it comes up for you while you're reading it. But do not force it.

- Slow down. There is definitely an art to performance that involves pacing and momentum but, for the most part, unless you are at a slam and literally under the clock, take your time with the piece.

- You have punctuated the poem for a reason. Bring those commas and periods to life by, you know, breathing. Or bring the exclamation points to life by exclaiming!

- Say your lines clearly. I had my real education in this when I did my first readings in Germany, and had to read my poems in English for an audience who did not share my mother tongue. They had some fluency, and could understand me, but only if I slowed down and enunciated. It taught me to do more than just slow down and get clear; it taught me to relish each line and its sounds. I felt like I was hearing my own work for the first time.

- Allow yourself to remember where you were at, mentally and emotionally, when you wrote the piece. Go there. Then let go. Get free. See what happens.

ASSIGNMENT

Is your blood sugar dropping? I think your blood sugar is dropping. Put down this book and make yourself a little something—slap together a sandwich, heat up some soup, get out the hummus! Homeostasis for all!

CHAPTER 16:
LESSONS FROM THE HANGED MAN – EDITING FOR CONTENT

Let's revisit the Tarot for a moment, to bring up the second-creepiest Major Arcana Card (after, of course, the Death Card): the Hanged Man. In the old-school Rider Deck, the hanged man is a picture of a hanging man, upside down, tied at the ankles to a tree. The tree is actually supposed to be a gallows, in the shape of a Tau Cross, which is a symbol with origins as far back as the Sumerian culture (that's Mesopotamia my friends, around 4500 –4000 BC), but these days is more commonly seen as an old Christian cross emblem standing (or hanging) for death, resurrection, and blood sacrifice. There is a crude glow around his head that is supposed to indicate, I think, that he is a holy martyr. The look on his face is a detached trance, not anguish, which supports the interpretation that he has tied *himself* to the goddamn cross, or allowed himself to be tied there, to hang forever, to rot, and to die.

In my James Wanless Voyager deck, the Hanged Man is a delicious collage of images that includes an encircled upside-down golden man statue, octopus tentacles, what I believe is a snaking piece of the Great Wall of China, a broken-off glass goblet stem, an inky black swirling whirlpool, what might be blood-red lotus petals, some hands cupping a dark mirror face in them, and a bunch of other things I can't even identify. Universal-Jungian-symbol-orgasm, like all his other cards. James posits that, "the Hanged Man symbolizes the law of reversal. As in the crucifixion of Christ, success is achieved in a manner opposite of what is expected. Instead of assertive movement and forceful resistance, salvation is obtained through passive surrender...When feeling hung up, encircled, netted and walled in, wait it out. Assume a holding pattern. You are in suspense, a limbo that demands you tread water. Accepting your limitations brings expansion."[29] He says some other insightful things, but we're going to come back to those later.

It's time to discuss editing for content, and it's time to face some Hanged-Man, blood-sacrifice-hard truths. As our old friend Chuck Wendig from the editing section invocation sums up so eloquently, "Creativity is dead without skill."[30] (If you are unfamiliar with Dr. Wendig, he is a gamer, novelist, screenwriter and prolific author of e-books on writing. Few people cuss more freely and say more mean things we all need to hear. He is our anti-Natalie Goldberg. Go buy all his stuff. He is writing mostly to aspiring novelists, but editing is editing.) Welcome to the tough love chapter. This is the chapter where I finally say to you: writing itself may be tricky, and require tricking ourselves into doing it, but writing *well* is hard. Really really hard. It is back-breaking, carpal-tunnel-inducing work to gain and hone your skills and execute them like the Jungian Sorcerers we have the potential to be.

It could take decades, or more, but unfortunately, "decades" is all we get, so let's get ON this. To get anywhere, we have to write, like, A LOT, and we have to write a lot of bad poetry. Allow me to repeat: we have to write a lot of poetry that is objectively, irredeemably bad. And we have to face facts along the way about where our skill level is actually AT. We have to own up to how it is holding us back (hanging us up) from achieving our perfect visions of glowing, pulsing, understandable, beloved poems. You and I still have a lot to learn, and that learning will only come from being honest about our limitations, dedicating ourselves to self-compassion about the whole walking-before-we-can-run thing, writing and editing our asses off, putting our whole backs into it, and for an indefinite, frustrating, Sisyphean length of time.

Tomas Tranströmer, who just won the Nobel Prize for his poems, is 80-years-old. He started writing earnestly and professionally in his twenties, which was in the 1950s. He has been writing for over sixty years, and has published over fifteen books. He suffered a debilitating stroke 22 years ago that left him partially paralyzed and unable to speak, and he *still kept writing*. His latest book of poems, *The Great Enigma*, was published just eight years ago, in 2004. He is inarguably a genius poet and deserving of the Nobel. But it took him a lifetime of writing to get there. We are crippled, whining, finless zygotes compared to him. We have brilliance in us, yes, but we lack Tomas' skill. And we are jealous, ego-bruised, and thwarted because the creativity monster is throwing an all-out I-want-it-now temper tantrum inside of us, and it is stressing us OUT and making us DEPRESSED, SELF-DOUBTING-THOMASES. Again, in elegant Chuck-speak, "High creativity: low skill. Sad trombone. Weepy panda."[30]

You are reading your pieces out loud now, and you are hearing/seeing many problems and, hopefully, taking notes and tracking them, not in your head but on paper (or your futuristic touch screen). These problems can be solved. These problems are opportunities to become more skilled writers. Without the bad writing, without the mistakes, without the problems and the conflict presented by needing to solve them, we will learn *nothing*. If we can identify the problems—especially our consistent problem areas and weaknesses—we can work at solving them. We can work to make it work: all the words singing in the same sound chorus, pushing the same metaphor up the same hill. We can make these suckers make sweet sense.

And of course: *how we do anything is how we do everything*. When you learn to identify any problem in any area of your life, force yourself to really examine it and SEE IT and accept its reality, apply yourself to finding a solution, and then FIX IT, you are not just becoming a better cook, a better amateur-electrician, a better negotiator with the bureaucracy at [fill in your favorite maddening bureaucracy here], you are also becoming a better writer. You are building necessary neuropathways of AHA!

Which brings up another point. Though you should be writing poetry, like, A LOT, you should also be doing other things, like working to earn money so you can pay your bills and eat, brushing your teeth, repairing your bicycle tires, taking that bike on rides, going to museums and shows, making rad birthday gifts for the people you love and its prequel activity, remembering the people-you-loves'-birthdays, and finally (to travel back to the first piece of advice in this whole book): reading. *Reading*. MORE READING! You should be reading every chance you get, and not just poetry or fiction or Alan Moore comics, but tons of non-fiction on fascinating topics. You will not damage your creative process by having a life outside of it. In fact, I am positive that's impossible. Your precious creative process is not located at your writing desk, or your favorite coffee shop, or your weird dirty rat's-nest writer's-den corner in the basement that is littered with candy wrappers and never-returned-to-the-library Tony Hoagland books and porn. It is wherever you are, happening all of the time. It needs both times of focus and concentrated work, and times of play and rest and space for it to function and evolve. It cannot be separated from you and all your activities.

And also, I will beat you over the head with this book in your hands if you do not start writing and often and with consistent discipline. Back to the *second* piece of advice in this book: work begets work. We will have nothing to edit if you are not out there writing steadily like the poetry-machine that you are or that I am forcing you to become. There is NO SUCH THING AS WRITER'S BLOCK. There is only procrastination and excuses. When you feel totally empty, when you think you having nothing to write, write anyway. You will surprise yourself. And the writing will create more writing. I know all of this smacks of impossible expectations and paradox— live your life, read all the time, write every day, take time off from writing to live, but keep writing all the time! But remember? Paradox is our new breakfast cereal. We thrive on it.

Ok. Back to the Topic topic: editing your poems for content. What do I mean, exactly, by the difference between editing for content, context, language and format? Well, guys, I admit, there is a ton of cross-over in all poetic territory. But you already know my approach to handling things like this. The topic of editing poetry is so big and complicated and impossible, I needed to randomly invent a structure. So, pretty arbitrarily, I am deciding that when editing for content you are looking for the following things in your piece:

- Consistency of voice: Does the whole poem sound like it is written by the same writer? AKA, you? (Unless you mean for it to be in several voices, and you are deploying typographical devices or punctuation correctly to indicate when you are in one voice or another and that, you know, makes *sense* in the context of the topic and structure of the piece you are working on.) (Oh God. This is already turning into a big, hot, there-are-no-rules-in-poetry mess.)

- Coherency of narrative or message: Does the poem make sense? Will readers be able to understand, with some work on their part encouraged and allowed, what you are talking about? This answer needs to be a resounding YES, even if it makes the kind of sense that is OUT THERE and messy and upsetting and leaves big confusing unanswered questions in their bellies for future digestion/indigestion. Did the poem have a message or story to tell, and did you get it across? Is there any part of the poem where you seem to tell a whole other story, and you didn't tie it back in in any way, indicating why it got included in the family photo? If so, get rid of it. Please.

- Cleanliness of metaphor: I only used "cleanliness" because things are getting so messy on this list, and I seem to be on a C-sprint. Does the poem have a guiding metaphor, or at least less than 10, and did you work that metaphor to the fullest? Did you stretch it and bend it and let your dog chew on it and make sure it was unbreakable? Did you weave it in and out of the poem, let it peek through all the cracks to wink at the reader? Does your imagery and vocabulary support that metaphor? Does the metaphor directly support, enhance and give a giant megaphone to your ultimate point?

- Credibility of intent: Does the content of this poem come from *your* Source, *your* perspective, *your* experiences? And if not, did you connect yourself to the topic, directly or indirectly, as a way of exploring why you are writing about it, and forging or revealing major connectivity in the universe? Does it feel like you wrote it? In your voice? Does it sound too much like someone else's poem or voice, and not intentionally? If so, you have a serious problem. You have been under the influence of another writer, and you should cut WAY back, scrap the whole thing and start from scratch.

- It's cut to its quick: You got your editing scissors out and cut out all the excess, expendable words and parts. Poems don't need operas of description, though we all love to get our soprano diva vocabulary aria on. (Like how I could have just written "vocabulary aria" without the extra descriptors and you would have gotten the exact same meaning?) Great poems use just enough of the right words, in the right combination, and together they mean many things, and their overall texture and meaning(s) do all the heavy lifting with their spindly little letter-arms. You cut as much as you could from the piece, without sacrificing crucial-to-your-message images and metaphors, and without compromising rhythm and musicality and flow. It is not too long; it is just long enough.

- The connotation police have swept the poem crime scene and found no evidence of foul play: You discovered all the parts where you explained rather than describing; you described rather than showing; you showed rather than indicating. You fixed it, and got your connotation and indication on. You let the readers use their imaginations and psychological projections. You didn't condescend and over-explain. You trusted them to read your piece, and to find all the clues you planted in it so that they might discover the buried treasure. That treasure *was* buried, and the reader had some digging to do, but you gave them a map. The map had a legend and a key and an arrow pointing North. It had a big red X, or several, maybe in the title, or the last line, or lots of places that, when tied together with mappy dashes, meant the-treasure-is-HERE. Here we go now, metaphors about metaphors about metaphors. Are you feeling woozy? Do you need to lie down? Or is it just me?

- Clarity of Amazingness: Finally: you wove some serious wisdom in to this poem, or some damn funny dialogue or irony that turned out to also be wisdom in trickster fox clothes, or really surprised yourself with your bravery and mad genius and creativity with structure and word play. This is the most important content edit. Do you love the poem? Are you thrilled that you wrote it? (You will know by your instant desire to share it immediately with others.) Will the poem make the reader want to read all your other poems? Does it shout, "I killed it!" without taking a bow, 'cause it didn't have to?

Some final words from the Hanged Man, and his interlocutor-of-my-choice James Wanless, on this whole poem-writing front. He wants to remind us that, often, we are under constrictive influences beyond our control. The key is to surrender your ego. (I can hear all the egos reading this, starting to plan my assassination. Hey egos —I can *hear* you guys. You are not real! You are not intimidating me! Give up the ghost!) If you are frustrated with your writing;

if you have gotten criticism and negative feedback about it, and it STUNG; if this whole process of writing and sharing your writing and not getting the validation you think you need or should get is making you feel ill, or depressed, or angry and persecuted, please, for the love of all that is holy, stop taking poetry and yourself so seriously.

And on a very serious note, "the feeling that you are drowning and being dragged to the depths" is what they mean when they say *dark night of the soul*. It is "but the preparatory stage for rebirth and new life and better work."[29] Keep the faith. Don't give up. Except your ego. You have to give that up or you will suffer and suffer and suffer and not learn anything or get better at writing. One last time to Chuck: "Be the scrappy underdog, not the self-assumed victor-of-Thunderdome."[30] Hear, hear Chuck Wendig, you master excess-scrapper, you crucifixion resurrection overlord of zombie fiction and all things-writing advice. I bet you're out there right now, wrestling the octopus tentacles of some brilliant new fiction, making us all look like charming, harmless sea anemones. (Oh, wait, that metaphor didn't quite work…aren't sea anemones predators? I should go look that up and consider editing it.)

ASSIGNMENT

Take three of your favorite poems by other authors, the ones you have been diligently collecting. They should be by different poets and have significant variance in voice and style. Put each poem through the wringer of the "content edit" questions in this chapter, and take notes. The answers will help you see in concrete ways why poems that work work. Why you love them. It will also point out how different writers handle content in different ways, and show you the infinity of choices at *your* disposal.

CHAPTER 17: THE LOST CHAPTER

Anxiety is the handmaiden of creativity. T.S. Eliot said that. I might have replaced "handmaiden" with "dominatrix" or "fire-breathing shadow of certain death." But he basically nailed it.

After editing my editing chapters, I realized something was missing from this discussion of the writing process. A certain percentage among us are *not* suffering from over-blown writer egos at all, but rather from mangling anxiety and crippling self-doubt. We hear criticism about our writing and internalize it instantly. We hear praise and are immediately suspicious. We love writing, but could not explain to anyone why, exactly, we love it, because clearly we are total masochists about it.

You must be searingly self-critical about your writing. You must practice honesty and radical self-acceptance about your limitations in order to spur you on to further mastery. And you should always be questioning your skills, asking whether a particular line or an entire poem has met its potential, or whether it works at all. But all this self-criticism can easily lead to total paralysis. And not the kind that advice like "begin anywhere" can fix.

Feeling lost, or stuck, or filled with anxiety about your work or your life is not just normal. It is a necessary part of the creative process. If the creative process were a predictable cycle, and it's not, the emotional life of a writer with respect to his or her work might look like this:

THE "CYCLE" OF INSPIRATION

ELECTRIC IDEA

flow

FORCED
DISCIPLINED
WRITING

FLEETING
SATISFACTION

EMPTINESS

DOUBT
UPON REREAD

ABANDONMENT
AKA "FINISHING"

MORE
EDITING

~~EDITINNG~~
EDITING

*!!G! REBELLION!

MADDENING
FRUSTRATION

EXISTENTIAL
DESPAIR...

SUDDEN
CLARITY

GOOGLING ONLINE
EDUCATION COURSES
IN ACCOUNTING

MORE
EDITING

SELF-LOATHING

MORE
FLEETING
SATISFACTION

checking out

HALF-HEARTED
EDITING

UNRELATED
REJECTION LETTER
ARRIVES

DEPRESSION

I am always making hand written signs to post above my writing desk. Most of them are mantras or direct orders, meant to serve a sort of cheerleading or drill sergeant function. A selection of these signs include: "BLOSSOMING IS HARD!" "DON'T GIVE UP!" "NO CHECKING OUT!" "YOUR WORK IS BEING STALKED BY A MURDEROUS MEDIOCRITY AND YOU MUST MURDER THE MURDERER!"

But lest you get the impression that I am always a brave and cheerful warrior, a full-time glitter witch, allow me to share some of the other signs that have appeared over my desk in the last year, scratched out in utter despair: "WHAT IS HAPPINESS ANYWAY?" "YOU BETTER BUY MORE TISSUES." (And my personal favorite---) "FOLLOWING YOUR DREAMS IS STUPID."

So if you are reading this book from the cold dirt floor of some rock bottom crippling anxiety, know you are not alone. Anxiety and panic and craziness come with the territory of writing and creating and editing your creations. The writers you admire the most, I promise, have their own harrowing dark valleys of self-doubt. Ray Bradbury is quoted widely as saying, "I wish you a wrestling match with your Creative Muse that will last a lifetime. I wish craziness and foolishness and madness upon you. May you live with hysteria, and out of it make fine stories...Which finally means, may you be in love every day for the next 20,000 days. And out of that love, remake a world." He sure knows how to make the whole hysteria thing sound romantic, right? But then again, Bradbury knew a thing or two about decorating an apocalypse. I really miss that guy.

We know better. The madness and hysteria of creative anxiety has all the romance of bashing your head against drywall.

Let's remember everything we have learned about the blessing and the curse of storytelling. We are capable of suspending our suffering. Let's take again Ms. Solnit's advice about dosing ourselves in equal parts confidence and self-doubt and practice moderation. And let's know this: conquering self-doubt has every bit as much to do with giving up the ego as conquering arrogance. Accept and surrender. Let's embrace wherever we are at on the emotional spectrum of muse-wrestling or the "wheel of inspiration," and decide right now not to linger too long with T.S. in the wasteland. No going out with a whimper.

ASSIGNMENT

If you are in the throws of depression and self-doubt about your writing, throw a pity party—a real one. Since you the quickest way to get passed this stage of the process is to accept it and fully surrender to it, why not do it with some style?

Just got a rejection letter? Heard some criticism you can't let of? Hate everything you've ever written as you approach a deadline? PITY PARTY TIME! Invite friends! Invent a drink called The Disappointment. Use blackberry juice so it stains everything. Make decorations, like paper chains from all your work you are disgusted with, or glitter-glue signs that read, "I SUCK!"

Or make it a solo party and burn copies of all your latest work in a ritual fire while howling at the stars. (I mean it when I say *copies*. Don't be an idiot! How you feel today about your work is not how you will feel tomorrow or next week or next year.)

The point is to ratchet it up a few hundred notches and get it out of your system. As long as you don't hurt yourself, or anyone else, or destroy property that doesn't belong to you, go nuts. I find a good screaming at the moon incredibly helpful. Others enjoy destroying personal possessions of great significance. If you turn up the volume on your self-pity to comic proportions, you might (gasp!) remember how to laugh at all of this. Your depression may burn out sooner, and you can get back on those horses and ride them in the direction of creative bliss.

And maybe the real takeaway isn't what you *should do* to handle your despair and self-doubt, it's what you *shouldn't do*: sit on the couch watching reality TV shows you don't even enjoy, or whatever behavior you engage in that equals "checking out completely." You should be as creative in experimenting with your emotional coping mechanisms as you are with your writing process. And throwing a little glitter on the situation never hurt anyone.

CAVEATS AND PLATO-NIC TECTONICS

So! Let's pass out the champagne and chocolate milkshakes! We have slain the dragons of our Egos. Let's skin those puppies and decorate our cloaks with their magical iridescent scales! Let's party like it's 1999 FOREVER!!!

HA! *Yeah, right.* We have not done that. That is seventh-level-lifetime-daily-repetitive-jujitsu. BUT, we are sincerely attempting to lay that burden down to rest. To sing it to sweet numb sleep. Every day. In our writing. And in every other aspect of our lives. Are you *with* me? Then, tough-love accomplished. We can now move on to glittery love—the kind of feel-good, self-compassion-love, the kind of poetry-love and word-love that will be a balm to our troubled poet souls as we get prepared to Kill Our Darlings for the greater good of The Poem.

The final three chapters will require, however, that you and I share meaning. (Someone once told me that, "All culture is shared meaning." That was you, Paul Apodaca, no?) As we have discovered so often since Plato and since reading this book, we are LOST if we do not share definition. So let's cut to the chase—the vocabulary chase (you're going to read and absorb this so fast, it will feel like running.). Let's make sure we are on the same page about what poetic/general-writing devices and forms are available to us as sorcerers; let's agree about what they are and what they mean. This is not just a vocabulary lesson. This is not Poetry 101. This is really important because these are the tricks we have up our sleeves, to deploy correctly or on-purpose incorrectly or just incorrectly, and to learn from our incorrect deployment, so we can develop hardcore writing SKILLS. I meant core writing skills. No, wait, I meant hardcore.

For this purpose, I have gussied up a pseudo-dictionary-style vocabulary list of poetic terms, devices and forms. To make it as easy-to-use as possible as a quick look-up guide, it is at the back of the book. If you know you are on solid ground with this already, explicit permission to skip reading it. But we are not in expert's mind while reading this book, are we? We are in beginner's mind, also known as Shoshin, a concept in Zen Buddhism that refers to having an attitude of openness, eagerness, and lack of preconceptions when studying a subject, even when studying at an advanced level, just as a beginner in that subject would. Remember these lessons? 1) Let go of your expectations (Chapter 5), 2) Disarm yourself (Chapter 7), 3) Suspend your disbelief (Chapter 8) and 4) Challenge your basic assumptions Chapter 11). I was Shosining you with those. So maybe ground yourself Zen style and just read those definitions already. I'll wait.

[Elevator music]

Are you back from the back? Fantastic.

We have now gone deep on editing our pieces for content, and grounded ourselves in a shared meaning of terms to discuss editing for context, language and form. And before we go there, just for kicks, and to show exactly how insane I feel even trying to discuss this in separate chapters, I thought I would illustrate in one visual shot how various poetic devices relate to context, language and form. Ladies and gentlemen and nerd-kink enthusiasts—a poetic Venn Diagram.

VENN DIAGRAM ILLUSTRATING THE POETIC DEVICE CLUSTERCUSS OF HOW IT'S ALL CONNECTED, MAN

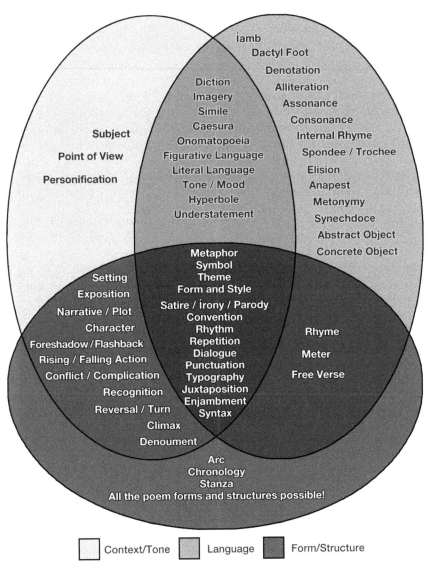

iamb
Dactyl Foot
Denotation
Diction   Alliteration
Imagery   Assonance
Simile   Consonance
Caesura   Internal Rhyme
Onomatopoeia
Figurative Language   Spondee / Trochee
Literal Language   Elision
Tone / Mood   Anapest
Hyperbole   Metonymy
Understatement   Synechdoce
                       Abstract Object
                       Concrete Object

Subject

Point of View

Personification

Metaphor
Symbol
Setting   Theme
Exposition   Form and Style
Narrative / Plot   Satire / Irony / Parody
Character   Convention
Foreshadow / Flashback   Rhythm   Rhyme
Rising / Falling Action Repetition   Meter
Conflict / Complication Dialogue
                         Punctuation   Free Verse
Recognition   Typography
Reversal / Turn   Juxtaposition
                         Enjambment
Climax   Syntax
Denoument

Arc
Chronology
Stanza
All the poem forms and structures possible!

Context/Tone   Language   Form/Structure

143

CHAPTER 18:
THE CURE FOR WHAT AILS US, WHICH MIGHT BE TONE DEAFNESS— EDITING FOR CONTEXT

Whether you are comfortable with this or not, being a writer means having something to say. You may not have known what that was back when you were dancing half-naked in the wild flowers of flow-land, writing whatever came out of you with no filter. Or maybe you did. Maybe you set out with absolute intentionality. It doesn't matter how you got here. You are now taking responsibility for turning this raw material into a poem, or writing this pretty-good poem into a much better poem. That means knowing *what* you want the poem to say so you can quality-control *how* it says it. And just to make it extra maddening, you have to do this in a way that leverages control over how a complete stranger is going to read it.

You have a literary-device arsenal at your disposal, but the one you need to cozy up to like a prison warden's key-ring is tone. Tone is your primary tool for communicating meaning. It is the thing that goes beyond denotation and connotation, the thing that transmits emotion. The tone or mood of your poem, the what you mean of what you mean, can be indicated in part with punctuation and syntax. A sentence that ends in an ellipsis is read entirely different from one that ends in a question mark or an exclamation point. But tone is largely built with context. A reader will decipher the intended tone of a word or line by what words or lines come before or after it.

Let's get example-y. The last lines of one of my poems in *Rise of the Trust Fall* read: "You would be amazed how much light there is./The stars stay out all night./Each snowflake is a mirror." Taken out of context, you can interpret only the surface meaning of these lines—that snow reflects light. Without knowing the title of the piece, or having read everything that came before it, how can you know if these lines are celebratory, or wistful, or dripping with sadness? I mean, this could easily be the end of a winter party poem.

But oh my, it is not. In fact, the end of this poem is kind of a heart-breaker. And you know this, because by the time you get there, I've given you all the context you need. You know the title, *To The Best Thing That Ever Happened To Me*. You know I have left someone after a fight, someone who wanted to marry me. I have run away and isolated myself in a snowdrift, and have realized I am trapped and rather doomed. You know I am reflecting on my instincts, on my behavior patterns, where they come from. You've also just read the preceding lines: "These are the soft frozen fields tundra vacations to./ The great white quiet./No one to distrust./I deserve this." Now the whole being-surrounded-by-snow-mirrors takes on a more haunting mood, no?

When I perform this piece, I nearly always put on Vince Guaraldi's instrumental version of *Christmastime Is Here*, from the soundtrack to *A Charlie Brown Christmas*, the saddest Christmas song *ever*. So I have a LOT of help setting up the mood, in addition to having my own tone-of-voice as an instrument to communicate the emotional meaning of the lines. But on the page, the words and their context have to do all the heavy-lifting. I need them to transmit shades of regret, a self-deprecating humor about my naivety and bravado, and the complicated mix of pain and sadness and relief with which we all eventually chew on the dead-ends of our self-fulfilling prophecies. Whether I am successful or not is something I will never really know. All this snowflake talk reminds me of good old Hans, telling us how we cannot know things for certain simply because we cannot observe everything. (You can decide if the poem succeeds for yourself, as the poem is up on my website www.thecultofmindy.com for you to read and judge at will.)

So the context in which you write and arrange your content will shape your tone, and this is crucial to communicating meaning. But this context thing gets even more important because your poems and their content do not exist in a personal vacuum. Words, ideas, images—they have history and symbolism and connotations galore. Remember Chuck's brilliant phrase, "hazy invisible cloud of context and possibility"? That is what is surrounding your poem.

There is a great argument to be made for just letting this context-control-thing go. After all, we actually have NO control over how our readers will perceive and interpret our work. We cannot force them, Vulcan-mind-meld-style, to see and understand things exactly as we do. Oh sweetjesus, if we could! We could quit right now. We could just wander around our towns and cities imparting our poems directly into people's heads with our spidering hands! (Wait—did someone give a TED talk already about how to do that? Did I miss it?)

But we are not lazy writers who give up on our goal of being gotten that easily. NO! We are crazy control freaks who want to be understood! We know this is our only hope, our only way out of this lonely, echoing head-cave, the only way to reach out and touch someone without touching them. (I looked it up just now—no such TED talk has been given yet.) And when I say *we* are crazy control freaks, I mean that *I* am, and that this whole discussion is about Control. Not just the maddening-when-unmet psychological need. I mean control as a real skill, a power over your powers. I mean it like the way that if you practice it often enough, and under low-stakes circumstances, you can eventually learn to speak your mind spontaneously and clearly on a *very* emotional subject for you, with a strong, even voice—even as the tears are building at their escape-hatch-ducts, even as your voice box is threatening tremble, even as every brain-stem-managed-muscle in your body is priming to run away, and fast, from this potentially devastating and traumatic emotional conflict.

Controlling tone is a real and learnable skill. So first of all, let's take a look at some of the questions we can ask ourselves about our poems that will help us in this quest.

What am I trying to say in this poem? Try to write it down in one sentence.

- I am trying to say that my father abandoned me, and now I don't trust men.

- I am trying to say that power corrupts, and that I feel corrupted by writing about it; I feel corrupted and confused about having it— power.

- I am trying to say that poodles are the best dogs. (They are the best dogs.)

How do I feel about this topic I am writing about? How is my reader supposed to feel?

- Should they feel my despair? Should they experience moments of solidarity and understanding and "mmhmmm girl"? Should they feel sorry for me/not sorry for me? Should they feel dark and hopeless about this, like I feel? Should they feel forgiveness and peace? Should they feel confident and optimistic, like healing and transformation is imminent for me?

- Should they feel anger and self-righteousness? Should they feel detachment and equanimity? Should they feel heady and inspired by new and complicated feelings and thoughts about the potential for evil and good within them?

- Should they feel pretty stoked about poodles, too? Because they don't shed, and the smaller ones are scoopable, and they are pretty smart and play with themselves well, and are the snuggliest? But I don't need to say all that; everyone already knows that about poodles. I just need them to feel my poodle joy.

Where in this poem did I succeed at hitting my aim, bulls-eye? What parts enforced and defended my vision? Where is my tone ringing loud and clear?

- Oh man, that setting of an empty train station. The amount of time I wait, uncomfortably, because the benches are hard and wooden and have no warmth. The part where I am putting my hands on the cold steel of the tracks to see if I can feel the rumbling of a far off train on its way, so I can know whether or not I should wait any longer. The way I describe train signals as sounding like my dad whistling happily in the shower, behind a closed door: perfect. The way I finally decide to leave the station and head back home and how, as I'm walking away, I stick my hand in my coat pockets and find cash I forgot was there. Zing!

- I personified those Wall Street skyscrapers so kickass! They are having these sneering conversations with one another, telling racist/sexist/classist jokes and sniggering and bragging and swagger-swaying in the head winds, one thousand feet up. I alternate between descriptions of them in the 1930s and the 1990s, and they complain about how their insides rot so quickly, the constant renovations they have to endure, like old men getting oral surgery to have their blackened teeth replaced by purchasing stolen porcelain and gold. They say they smile like horny sweaty teenagers again now. Gross!

- I describe a poodle as the best cloud I can ever remember seeing: it was so fluffy and it did not move; it just floated serenely in the bluest sky. It stayed still so long I could easily project myself on to it, pretend I was hanging out on it and feeling really happy. It was so comfy I fell asleep on it, by which I mean on the bed of grass I was looking at it from, all stretched out for the summer afternoon, and didn't wake up until it neared twilight, and started to rain lightly, and the rain tickled my face, and I work up just in time to see the finish of a simple, sweet sunset.

Conversely, where did I miss the target entirely? Where do I veer off-course and not-on-purpose? Which words do not belong to this tone, this intention, this overall meaning-aim? What is missing from the poem?

- Crapsticks! There's a whole part in there where I want to call my clearly-male lover to come pick me up but my phone booth is broken. It seemed like a good frustration metaphor at the time, but doesn't that indicate I do trust men? Also, I describe the clocks at the station all wrong. I make it seem like they're "watching" me and rooting for me. That doesn't feel right. They should be detached, clockwork-universe-theory indicators, indifferent Gods, underscoring my theme of my feelings unseen and uncared for by my father.

- WAA-waaaaa. I didn't connect myself to the skyscrapers and their conversation AT ALL. I wanted to implicate that I was scared of becoming one of them, to highlight my idea about my own fears about being corrupted by my blossoming power. Should I be a new building being built by a new architect, over-hearing their conversation? Could I describe my architect as a nervous, high-strung man, chewing his pen caps, worrying about the massive amounts of money he's making to build this stupid skyscraper when all he ever wanted to do was build weird museums?

- Nope. Totally nailed it with the poodle poem.

So. We've read our poems. Out loud. We are firmly rooted in knowing what we want them to mean, and say. We've asked the hard questions, and edited them, and tracked where we succeeded and where we failed. We noticed what didn't belong, and what was missing. Maybe we need to go back now and add some connective tissue. Maybe we need to experiment with switching points-of-view, rewriting them from that angle, then checking in again about how they sound and feel now in that different voice. Maybe we need to do that several different times, in several different ways. Maybe our word choices can be fixed. Maybe we can come up with more-fitting, better-tailored images. Maybe we can play around with being more or less direct, or more or less figurative. Maybe we can swap out our weaker, limper symbols with stronger heavy-lifter-y ones. Maybe we can really jazz up the descriptors of the setting, or objects in the scene, to more closely hone in on our intended mood and tone. Maybe we should have gotten way more abstract? Maybe we should have grounded this piece in more concrete details? Maybe we should go get our thesauri out. (I know I could have chosen to say "thesauruses" just then. But I like to imagine my thesaurus as a Pegasus. And Pegasus HAS NO PLURAL because, I guess, it's not a real thing, it's a name. But the general usage on the streets for the plural of Pegasus is Pegasi. So I went with "thesauri." Deal.)

And maybe—*maybe*—we should (Egads!) just crumple the poem up into a paper snowball of shame and throw it away, and start from scratch. Enter poem-editing-guru Tony Brown again for some much needed advice. I fell in poet-love with Tony Brown a long time ago. He lives in Worcester, Massachusetts, as do many of my other favorite poets and old friends. (Hi Victor! Hi Lea!) But I first became obsessed with Tony as a process guru when I heard he was on a mad one-year sprint to write, like, 500 poems or something. And he *did it*. By, like, November. (I don't know for sure what the number was that first year. But I know that over the course of two years he wrote over one thousand poems. OVER ONE THOUSAND POEMS! THERE IS NO SUCH THING AS WRITER'S BLOCK!) My obsession was nurtured further still when I heard that he had then declared a "Year Of Editing," during which he would write NO new poems and just grapple with the massive pile that had accumulated from his jaw-dropping prolificness. I love when people experiment with these kinds of extremes. It's incredibly inspiring and humbling. He is also serious with his Benjamin Franklining. He documents all of his poetic output and efforts shamelessly on a public blog called "Dark Matter," located at radioactiveart.wordpress.com.

So I first asked Tony one simple question: what's the best advice you've ever been given about editing. And he replied, "I don't know who gave it to me, or where I got it or when, but the best advice I ever received is simply, 'Be ruthless.'" Yes Tony! We are trying! We have drugged our fragile egos into temporary comas and are trying to toughen up as writers and editors to do what William Faulkner suggested and *kill our darlings*. We are trying to be fearless and egoless about excommunicating our most favorite images and phrases when they do not serve at the pleasure of the poem.

Tony also advises us to take a lot of breaks from our poems. Let them sit. Let them stew, and ferment, and just breathe for awhile without our constant and oppressive surgeons' eyes watching them. But I think the greatest, most important idea he imparted to me was this. I'm just going to let him say it.

> "I've been at this poetry thing for close to 40 years now (I'm now 52 and had the moment of clarity by age 12-13 or so that I was going to be a poet, no matter what else happened to me in life). It took me a long time to understand that what matters most is The Work—the entire body of work over time. That any one poem is less relevant to the Work than the full body of poems itself.
>
> So editing, revising one poem, maybe even to the point of discarding it (which I have done more than once), is less painful to me than betraying The Work itself—the Work of having all the poems, over time, tell a story about me and my world and my reaction to it and my understanding of it that no one poem can do on its own.

Once I accepted that—and it took a long time; I think it was maybe only 10 years ago or so, concurrent with my retirement from slamming—ruthlessness in the editing process of a single poem became far more OK with me. My stubbornness over hanging onto any given line really fell away when seen in the context of the Work. As long as the process pulled me farther along the path toward what I wanted from the Work in the long run, I'd go there.

After all, I can always write another poem."

Are you listening readers? Because I am. I am not deaf, and I am not tone-deaf, and neither are you: *you can always write another poem*. This is an incredibly hopeful statement. It is dripping with phoenix tears. It is filled with possibility, and regenerative magic, and holy holy confidence, not in one's genius, but in one's Self and one's Work as something that could be greater than the Self, if you gave it the chance. If you put your back into it.

We are travelling on a life-arc of growth and self-actualization, yes, but there's something even greater we can reach for—the actualization of our unique vision of what is missing for us in this world through our art. So to hell with our darlings! We are darling machines. We will always be drowning in darlings. We have some stories in us, and maybe it's just one story masquerading as many stories. We are going to try to tell that story over and over and over again until we get it right. Until it is a small, perfected, time-and-elements-smoothed stone, thrown in the great pond of the IS. Skipping in its impressive anti-gravity stone-dance. Then plopping down into the depths, leaving behind only those expanding circles in the water: the rings and rings and rings.

ASSIGNMENT

Pull a Tony Brown! Wait. That's way too much pressure. Pull a half-Tony, or a one-twelfth Tony. Declare a month of editing, a month when you will take all of the work you've produced and rewrite and rework and reimagine. When you are editing, take extra care to edit for tone and context and not just content and language and form. And don't just look at the context within a single piece. Look at the collective context of the tone and narrative and meaning of all your poems, read together as a body of work. (Did I just challenge you to do the first steps to putting together a new manuscript?)

CHAPTER 19:
THE DARK SIDE OF THE RAINBOW— EDITING FOR LANGUAGE

Oh Gods and Goddesses of Poetry, Oh Monarchs of the Language Meaning Universe, I humble myself before you in prayer. My palms are clasped in reverence. My head and body are bowed and folded into the position of the infant in the womb. If you would allow me to be your unassuming servant of light and knowledge, I would burst with golden hummingbirds of gratitude. May you imbue me with your awesome powers of AHA! and Yes-That's-IT and OMFG! May there be no interruption or disconnection in our flowing helix of information infinity. May I accomplish my holy task. Amen. Aho. Nezdrovia.

I needed to start this chapter with a prayer. Not just because we are entering poetic-holy-grail-territory. But because it is Full Moon Friday. And not just any Full Moon Friday—today is Good Friday, the commemoration day of the crucifixion of Christ, and the first day of the Paschal Triduum. Even the upright Roman Catholic clergy traditionally begin this day, of all days, prostrate, in front of the altar. And even if I didn't care about any of that, it is a FULL MOON *and* it is a FRIDAY. The Greek word for Friday, *Paraskeviand*, is derived from a word meaning "to prepare" (παρασκευάζω). We need to empty our cups for this. We need to prepare to be filled with dark rainbow light.

For those of you who did not recognize the reference in the title of this chapter, you have inadvertently failed a very significant cultural literacy test in Contemporary Art and Media Studies. "Dark Side of the Rainbow" refers to the coincidental but synchronistic pairing of the 1973 Pink Floyd album *The Dark Side of the Moon* with the 1939 film *The Wizard of Oz*. You should maybe go handle a little quick research on YouTube. Now. There is a great tradition of dark-side-of-the-rainbowing amongst our people. If you are going to attempt to do this at home, be aware that there is some controversy as to whether to start the synchronicity at the appearance of the MGM lion, or the third roar, or the second or the first; others suggest starting the album not immediately after the lion's roar, but after the lion fades to black—exactly when the film begins. And, in general, if you have not listened to Pink Floyd's *The Dark Side of the Moon*, repeatedly, and to great hypnotic exultation/exhaustion, well, I don't what to say. The rest of this conversation may be lost on you.

In *Dark Side of The Rainbow*, the very moment Dorothy opens the door to walk out into Oz—to see a brand new world in Technicolor for the first time—track five, "Money," begins. The song opens with tape loops created by splicing together Roger Waters' recordings of clinking coins, tearing paper, a ringing cash register, and a clicking adding machine. The pairing of those sounds and Dorothy's first peek at the cash-lush foliage of Munchkin Land and the coin-gold Yellow Brick Road—it's a poet-musician-Jungian-psychologist-psychonaut's dream-come-true.

Ladies and gentlemen and total scoundrels of my readership, to prepare ourselves for a study of the center of our art form—language—the time has come for us to enter the realms of the truly primitive and religious. ("Tread warily, O prophet, when you move on to primitive religious ground."[31]) We need to reach back and explore the origins of all human awareness, the flash of consciousness that meteored our species from club-wielding Homo sapiens to brainy, existentially depressed, chronically elated philosophers, gaping at the stars and seeing, finally, patterns. It's time for us to enter Psychedelia.

Our guide for this journey will primarily be the acknowledged authority on the subject and the sincerest of American curanderos, Timothy Leary, author of the quote above. His book, *High Priest*, which chronicles his experiments with psychotropic drugs in and around Harvard University in the early 1960s, is nearly as important as his tome, *Tibetan Book of the Dead*. Add them to your list. But first, for the uninitiated in this general subject matter, some brief history.

Something happened in our human evolution that transformed us from our prehistoric mammalian state, from our primal hunter-gatherer beginnings, into beings that could think, reflect, imagine, dream and invent. This catalyst is commonly believed, in both secular-scientific and many mystical traditions, to have been the psychedelic mushroom. How else, we must ask ourselves, can we explain our sudden advancement as a species into exploring and forging the realms of math, language, art, organized society—culture itself?

Imagery discovered in primitive cave murals in the areas of modern Spain and Algeria suggests that the human use of mushrooms dates back to many thousands of years ago.[32] In Mesoamerica, mushrooms have a long history of being consumed in spiritual and divinatory ceremonies. Spanish interlopers documented these traditions as early as the 16th century. And maybe you did not know this, oh-those-of-us-who-were-raised-under-the-government-proclamation-of-Just-Say-No, but in the late 1950s, after Swiss chemist Albert Hoffman isolated the active compound psilocybin, his employer, the multinational pharmaceutical company Sandoz, began mass-marketing and selling world-wide pure psilocybin to physicians and clinicians for use in psychedelic psychotherapy. It wasn't until increasingly restrictive FDA regulations and drug laws were passed in the 60s to curb this scientific research that the mushroom's general perception and use as an ethogen (a spiritually enhancing agent) grew in popularity. Oh, the unintended consequences of laws and regulations! Enter Dr. Leary, Harvard professor of psychology, psychedelic drug advocate, and dissident visionary.

Leary believed, whole-heartedly, in the potential for LSD and psilocybin as therapeutic agents. He's the radical who coined and disseminated the catchy phrases: "Turn on. Tune In. Drop out." and, "Think for yourself and question authority." Those phrases or ideas are so idiomatic in English language and culture now, it is difficult to imagine a time when they didn't exist. His research led him to propose an "eight-circuit model of consciousness," attempting to unify into one meta-theory various hypotheses on the mind and its alterations of state. He was inspired not just by psychology, neurology, sociology, anthropology, physics, chemistry, biology, mathematics, and religious systems (both Western and Eastern *and* including Freemasonry); he was inspired by the Hindu chakra system, and by the tenets and practice of yoga.

Leary's umbrella theory posits that eight different neurological circuits, each corresponding to specific states of consciousness, exist, at least in some latent form, in all of us.[33] The first four reside in the left hemisphere of the brain, and are responsible for basic survival functions: subsistence, emotion, communication, sexuality, politics and morality. The last four reside in the right hemisphere, and are more "cerebral" (figuratively speaking) and are dedicated to aesthetics, states of ecstasy, self-analysis, philosophy and spirituality—one's relationship to the Universe. He believed the last four were more recent brain-circuitry developments, evolutionarily speaking, but were becoming increasingly vital for our survival as a species. (Vaclav Havel's haunting warning comes to mind: "Transcendence as the only real alternative to extinction.") He believed we could activate these last four systems or circuits by using psychedelic or psychotropic drugs, neuro-linguistic programming (NLP), Crowleyan magick, meditation, and, of course, yoga.

But let's forget Leary's fascinating theories for a moment and just focus on the psychedelic mushroom: what ingesting psilocybin DOES to us. Without getting all Chapter 15 on you, I want to explain that what the drug actually does in your body is mimic the action of the delicious, multi-tasking neurotransmitter serotonin. Specifically, it acts as a post-synaptic S-HT$_{2A}$ receptor agonist. (For you fellow aspiring science-nerds, S-HT$_{2A}$ is a specific form of 5-Hydroxytryptophan, and is the link between the serotonin neurotransmitter and the L-tryptophan amino-acid. An agonist is any chemical that binds to a receptor of a cell and triggers a response by that cell.) Psilocybin ingestion also causes an indirect effect—increasing concentrations of dopamine in the basal ganglia. (Do NOT get me started on the wondrous basal ganglia. Have you ever imagined that there is a tiny serious person in your brain, attending 24/7 to your operations at a sort of spaceship console by monitoring various colorful screens of information and pulling levers and pushing giant glowing buttons? Well, you were basically right. Basal. Ganglia.)

There are many "positive" effects of this subversion and disruption of your normal neurotransmitter- amino-peptide interaction. It drastically changes your perceptions of the world around you and within you, causing euphoria, visual and mental and auditory hallucinations, and distorting your sense of time and space. In a nutshell, it's pure poetry projected and personified in harmonic, pulsing unification all around you, except there is no "You" that is separate from the external everything and everywhere. Negative side effects include nausea (and its disgusting child, puking-your-guts-out) and, very commonly, panic attacks.

This reminds me of a funny (to me) story from my college days, when I was always living communally (and thus affordably) in houses in various stages of chaos and disrepair with many roommates. One day, one such roommate and a friend decided to split an entire eighth-ounce of mushroom. Depending on potency, that can be, like, A LOT. The friend was your classic Carlos-Castanedian, California-spiritual, eco-political surfer-dude type. He was ready to "Turn on. Tune In. Drop out." He was prepared to do it through chanting, meditation, incense, specially curated artwork, and intentional self-spelunking deep down into the unlit, dark-crystal-lined caves of his psyche. The roommate was a good-looking, charismatic Theater Major. This means he spent nearly all of his time and energy either trying to get laid or perfecting the art of believably Being Someone Else. The roommate wigged the fuck out.

I was alone in the house with them, and they had forewarned me of their trip intentions, so I emerged from my bedroom when I heard the beginnings of psychotic wailing and rending and sobbing. I found my roommate in a state of complete physical and mental agitation, crunched into a tense ball on the hardwood floor of the dining room. When he saw me, he grabbed my legs and, real tears of anguish streaming down his reddened face, began screaming at me. "I don't know how to FEEL!!!" he cried repeatedly. "Tell me HOW to FEEL!!!" I grabbed him squarely by the shoulders, made full-laser-eye-contact with him, and then said loudly and slowly and clearly: "YOU ARE ON DRUGS. YOU WILL EVENTUALLY COME DOWN." But he was already too far gone, hurtling towards the Peak. Apprentice-shaman-surfer-dude looked at a total loss—for language, for gestures, for any connection to this fresh monster. Not wanting to babysit temporary lunatics for the next five hours, but concerned for the safety of the entire neighborhood, I went to my bedroom, found some spare poster board, wrote with red Sharpie in big bold capital letters, "YOU ARE ON DRUGS / YOU WILL EVENTUALLY / COME DOWN," taped it to the living room wall, locked them in the house, and left.

As usual, I digress. I want to make very clear that I am NOT suggesting you go out and get yourself some hallucinogens and take them so that you can become a better writer. I am suggesting a lot of Other Things. Like there is nothing psilocybin can do to our brains that they don't already have the natural capacity to do and potential for doing. And that to create fresh, Technicolor-vivid images and descriptors that will capture our reader's attention and imagination, we need to get psychedelic with our process. We need to free ourselves from all our stiff, uptight, dogmatic training about "how words are supposed to be used." We need to be open to radical, new, synesthetic perceptions of the world around us. We need to detach ourselves from standard experiences of time and space. We need to "hallucinate" within our own minds, projecting onto their blank screens characters and places and things and events that are not concrete or "real." This is also commonly referred to as *daydreaming*. We need to lucidly daydream. This is how we prepare to write and edit the language in our poems—to get in there like psychedelic surgeons. We need to SEE and HEAR and SMELL and TASTE and FEEL and INTUIT the connections between all words and things with full, pulsing, tracering clarity.

There *are* ways to trick ourselves into getting this loose in the head. This is what free-association exercises are all about. It's everything I've been talking about and hinting at all along in this book and readying us for. Now, you bought (or stole or borrowed) this book wanting to get some concrete advice, not a fuzzy lesson in the hows of hallucinating. Here's what I got:

1. PERFORM CONCRETE OBJECT PERSONIFICATION EXERCISES

Rachel McKibbens reappears to offer one of the best exercises I've ever seen taught for poetic-mind self-trickery. She came up with this exercise when she was working for several years at Bellevue Hospital, conducting creative-writing workshops with youth incarcerated there because doctors had diagnosed them with a variety of serious, potential-for-real-harm, mental illnesses. (We love to pathologize all non-conformist behavior, and that is all I'm going to judgmentally say on that subject.)

What Rachel has her students do is draw three columns on a piece of paper. The first column is labeled "Concrete Objects." She then has them make a list of concrete objects—chair, telephone, wedding ring, etc. Then she labels the next column "Animals." She asks them to write down the first animal they can think of that reminds them of that object. She asks them to think of the shape of the object, the size, the color, the smell, the taste, the sound, the usage—anything, and to not over think it. Then they must assign an animal to each object—elephant, songbird, beetle. Then she labels the third column "Behaviors and Aspects." She asks them to write down in that column what those animals do, or what they are known to be like—elephants are big and heavy, they lumber, wade into pools, forget nothing, mourn their dead; songbirds sing, trill, fly, and mate; beetles scuttle, scratch, are iridescent and glisten, and have hardened shell-like wings that protect them from being easily crushed.

Rachel then asks the students to dismiss, for a moment, the middle column, and to write phrases with the concrete objects as the subjects and the animal-behavior-aspect descriptors as the verbs and adjectives. This exercise produces magical, poetic phrases like, "the chair sat heavily, had waded into dark murky waters of the living room to mourn; it remembered everything." Or, "the phone trilled its mating song; the voice inside of it waited, trapped, frustrated with fresh love, desperate to fly." Or, "the hard diamond of her wedding ring scratched her maiden name lightly on to the glass of the window pane; it glistened iridescently in the sunlight as it did its cursive work, a ritual to remind herself of what could be broken and undone easily, and what could not. " BAM. Go do this exercise.

2. COLLECT WORDS

Many writers do this: they collect words and phrases and images and ideas they happen upon and fall in like or love with, and they put them into lists, and they lock these lists away in notebooks and computer Word document files for future use. Anytime you hear or read a word or phrase or idea or entire quote that you like the sound or meaning of, put it on the list. Anytime you hear or read a phrase or word or idea you do not understand, put it on the list, and resolve to look it up later and educate yourself. (Does anyone else out there just *love* the Rosalind Russell version of the film Auntie Mame? Besides its aesthetic Technicolor value, and besides the undeniability of Rosalind Russell, there is a very charming interaction in the opening scene, after Mame's nephew, Patrick, has been delivered to her house following the death of his father. He has walked right in to a busy bohemian cocktail party—classic Mame—and he keeps hearing words in the adult conversations that bewilder him. He politely pesters Mame to explain, and she hands him a notebook and pen and tells him to write down anything he doesn't understand, and tells him she will explain it later. When he presents her his list, he says, "Libido, inferiority complex, stinko, blotto, free love, bathtub gin, monkey glands, Karl Marx...is he one of the Marx Brothers?" HEART.)

3. MAKE SWEET LOVE TO YOUR DICTIONARIES

Did you know there are lots of different kinds of dictionaries? Of course you did. There's the omnipotent red brick Merriam-Webster classics. There are specialized dictionaries just for specific subjects. There are rhyming dictionaries, idiom dictionaries, and homonym dictionaries (which often include expertise on the homonym children homophones and homographs, as well as polysemes, heteronyms, and capitonyms). There are thesauri! These are your lovers. Spend a lot of time with them. Seek their attention and advice when you have a problem, or a strange dream. This is how you will become a meaning and sound guru.

4. MAKE NEW WORDS

You can do it! You have already done it! You will do it for as long as you live and breathe and write! Be daring! Be weird! Turn your nouns into verbs, your verbs into adverbs and adjectives, your adjectives into nouns. Use your new favorite tools Contraction and Portmanteau. If you cannot find the right word for what you are trying to say, *invent a new word.*

5. EUPHONY IS YOUR NEXT VACATION DESITINATION, AND YOUR FULL TIME JOB

This is an exercise in sensuality. You need to get really sensual about your words. You need to find sounds and words and word combinations that please you, that are like [insert favorite dessert here] to you. You are seeking harmony and avoiding cacophony (unless you are writing a poem about punk rock or having a heart attack. Then go nuts with the cacophony.). Your new friends for this are homonyms, alliteration, assonance, consonance, and internal rhyme, among others.

6. READ STUFF AND LISTEN TO MUSIC TO ABSORB THE WHATS AND HOWS AND WHYS OF RHYTHM

Your language should possess rhythm as well as rhyme (well, not rhyme necessarily, but all the things I noted in Step 5). Your teachers for this will be great writing of all genres and pretty much all types of music. Study and practice their use of meter, beat, repetition and turn for the purposes of mastering rising action, momentum, caesura, falling action, and resounding, satisfying denouement.

7. MANDALIZE YOUR MIND

You need to study symmetry, visual, auditory and linguistic symmetry. It could also be called mirroring, or reflective repetition. You can use intentional symmetry/asymmetry or imagery mirroring or repetition in your poems to underline meaning, or to create balance in the piece, or to write an ending or beginning, or to tie in all the stuff in the middle to the beginning and the end. Traditionally, Mandalas are concentric diagrams having spiritual and ritual significance in Hindu and Buddhist Tantrism. In Jungian psychology, the mandala is a symbol representing the effort to reunify the self. To me, they look like those art projects we made in elementary school with crayon shavings, wax paper, and irons. Mandalizing in poetry (I just made up that verb for this specific meaning) helps create cohesive pieces with unifying, harmonizing sounds and meanings, induces pleasing psychological projection and reflection in the reader, and maps the way to recognition, understanding and epiphany.

8. PRACTICE INTEGRITY

Let's resolve to always say what we mean and mean what we say. Total integrity. Total intention to facilitate cooperation and consensus amongst our feelings, thoughts, behaviors and words. Let's resolve to break open our poems and their word-chains and our Selves—dark night of the soul, dark side of the rainbow—and sew them back together, heal and smooth their stitches and scars, and make them WHOLE. Rainbows are discs, everyone! They are complete, circular discs of chromatically chronological, electromagnetic-spectrum light waves. In human-built rainbows of language, AKA poems, this wholeness contains the light and the dark, the colors you can see and the ones you cannot see. The pot of gold at the end of the rainbow (in the middle of it?) is all the colorful vocabulary you have been seeking. If you seek it with integrity of purpose, trust you will reach the gold.

ASSIGNMENT

I could throw something huge at you right now. I could tell you to invent one new word every day for the next year. Or to take all of your poems and change their nouns to verbs. Or to go memorize the dictionary. But that all sounds like a lot of work. Let's have some fun instead.

Select one of your favorite collections of poetry. Scan it to discover the twenty most commonly used words or images, or the ones that stand out the most to you—in this book you would perhaps find heavy doses of blood, glitter, vivid, mirror, shadow, snowflake, spark, dark, emerald, etc. Now write twenty lines, wherein each has to use at least three of the words. "The vivid sparks of your eyes are cheap emeralds of lust." "You dirty snowflake, you dark mirror—you are glitter shadow and wet spark." "When the money is gone, we will stalk the dark, glittering emerald mirrors, spending our smiles on the vivid."

This can get ridiculous. And surprisingly beautiful. And then ridiculous again. It will remind you how silly and awesome wordplay can be, how many ways you can yogalates the same twenty words into meaningless or meaningful poetry.

CHAPTER 20:
AWKWARD GRADUATION SPEECH—
EDITING FOR FORM AND STRUCTURE

I have already said nearly everything I wanted to say about the excitement and pitfalls of structure and form way back in Chapter 9. So let's just say I'm doing this last editing chapter as a *formality*. (Go on. Groan away. I am unashamed of my punning.) I am pretty dedicated myself to lawless free-verse writing. I get concerned at poetry readings whenever someone announces that they are about to read a series of sonnets, or pantoums on [insert heavy subject matter here]. I start eyeing the exits, battling an inner war with my Iowan politeness and my desire to get OUT of there. On the other hand, I am incredibly, irreversibly delighted when I hear or read a contemporary poem that handles a traditional form deftly, with mad-jealousy-inducing skill to make the form work and enhance, rather than detract or distract from, the theme. But still, I cannot imagine lecturing you for several pages on editing for form and structure when I, myself, am in a near-constant state of rebellion on this topic. Or can I…

[Sudden, unexpected fade in to a scene]

EXT. COLLEGE FOOTBALL FIELD – AFTERNOON

[A graduation ceremony has been set up on an enormous football field turned with perfectly manicured Bermuda grass. There is a large stage set up at one end. Many authoritatively robed professors and deans and other officials in their various, customized-to-denote-rank regalia are seated in cushioned seats, in rows, behind an imposing wooden podium. The graduating class is also wearing robes and funny tussled hats. They are legion. They are all sitting on uncomfortable folding chairs. The afternoon sun is angling just right to hit them square in the eyes, making those who forgot to wear rad shades squint and tear. A third of the graduating class is already drunk and wearing serious party attire under their robes. A few have chosen to be completely naked underneath them, for fraternity-kicks.

They are very antsy. Cash gifts, rich delicious meals, elaborate cakes and copious cocktails await them. And they have worked very long and very hard for this day—they have slaved in libraries and classrooms and at computers for years, hardly sleeping. They just want this diploma show to be OVER already, so they can move on to the next phase of their lives.

MINDY is announced as the final speaker before the officiating begins.
MINDY has been asked to give a speech on the most boring, inappropriate
subject ever chosen for a graduation ceremony—poetic forms. MINDY is so
nervous she does not hear them introducing her, and the enrobed stranger to
her right has to nudge her when the introduction has finished, and folks are
golf-clapping, and it is time for her to speak. As she approaches the podium,
she begins sweating profusely. Her hands betray her and tremble. She can feel
the graduates' disdain and impatience wafting off them in heady, woozy-ing
waves; a negative reflection of the sunlight off their cheap, black, hallowed
robes.

She tests the microphone a bit, and it causes a sharp shriek of feedback. She
looks panicked to stage left, at CRAIG the sound guy, who is furiously
adjusting levels. She fumbles awkwardly with her notes, soaking them with
palm grease, causing the ink on them to smudge.]

MINDY: Um, hi guys. So. I've been asked to say a few words about—um—
poetry forms. About their origins from many cultures. About their correct
usage. And about why you should all care deeply about resurrecting them
in your own writing, for, um, those of you who are writers out there. My,
uh, apologies, um, to the Business and Economics Majors, and those of you
earning your Bachelors of Science degrees today, as this topic will probably be
difficult for you to connect to, you know, *at all*.

[MINDY shifts uncomfortably for a second. Not only are her notes becoming
increasingly unreadable as their ink reacts to the sweat, but she realizes
she does not even have all her notes with her, and that she forgot to put on
deodorant this morning, and her Spanx are riding up.]

MINDY: So, right. Poetry forms. Let's see. We have the sonnet! You guys are
all familiar with the sonnet, right, from your studies of Shakespeare?

[The graduate crowd and their extensive guests begin to audibly murmur,
ignoring MINDY entirely. They chat with their neighbors, get up to greet
friends in other rows, order pizzas on their cell phones, pass around flasks.
MINDY makes a spur-of-the-moment decision.]

MINDY: You know what? Fuck this. Pardon my French. I'm a preacher's
daughter. If you guys want to know about the origins, historical and cultural
significance, and rules for executing poetry forms, you can go look them up.
There's some pretty aesthetically unpleasing websites out there on just this
thing. If you are moved to tears by William Blake or Elizabeth Browning, you
should just go study them, and their poems and their forms, in all the spare

time you will have while looking for jobs in this economy. Let's just switch topics entirely.

[The previously composed professors behind the podium now begin to murmur and ruffle. Someone is trying to signal someone about what the signal will be to pull MINDY off the stage.]

MINDY: What I want to talk about, instead, is the power of creativity, design and invention. Hey—Craig, that's your name, right? Can you cue me up some background music? I left you my iPod. Maybe some Explosions In The Sky? Off the Friday Night Lights soundtrack?

[CRAIG looks up from the soundboard. He has a ponytail and a Red Sox cap on. He gives MINDY "the nod" and the three fingers signal, meaning, she thinks, *just give me three seconds*. CRAIG is ON it. Soft, sweeping Americana guitars begin playing sweetly; they are filled with the emotions of innocence lost, nostalgia, hope.]

MINDY: That's much better. You're the creamsicle Craig, thank you.

[The graduate crowd laughs a little. They are slowly but surely turning forward in their seats to face the stage. They are paying attention.]

MINDY: Let's dig deep in to a little Bruce Mau ya'll. His book *Massive Change* begins, "For most of us, design is invisible. Until it fails. In fact, the secret ambition of design is to become invisible, to be taken into the culture, absorbed into the background. The highest order of success in design is to achieve ubiquity, to become banal."[34-begin] I love that word, banal. Onomatopoeia alert! Did that quote sound banal? Well, it's not. Everything you take for granted as natural in your lives, that you feel actually entitled to—freeways, cell phones, computers, printed books—were, at one point, carefully, thoroughly designed. They were brand new ideas. They revolutionized the world. It is only during a crisis or natural disaster or breakdown in these designs that we briefly and fleetingly become aware of their importance to us, how dependent we are on them, how helpless and clueless we would be without their foundation in our lives, these underlying systems of design.

Many of you will soon be getting into cars to drive somewhere, or planes to fly to vacations or new lives in new cities. Unless you are burdened with intense phobias, you will be blissfully unaware of the complex mechanisms involved in these machines you travel in, how your very survival depends on them working correctly. As long as there's no problem, you can just crank up the tunes and enjoy the ride.

This whole world is intricately interconnected. We walk around in private bubbles of isolated, individual experience and thought and emotion, believing we are disconnected from it all. Believing, perhaps, even that we are alone in this world and totally insignificant. But we are connected to everyone and everything—through the air we breathe, through the tools we use daily that, whether we can comprehend it or not, were built by hand, by someone else's hands, somewhere in a factory far far away.

We face profound challenges in this world, and in our lives. We often feel overwhelmed by them, paralyzed by ignorance or learned helplessness or by a very real inefficacy created by the systems of power that invisibly surround us and tame us. We ask ourselves, "Who am I, to think I can make a difference? That I can improve in any way this huge clusterfuck mess in any real lasting way?"

[Even the professors giggle at that F-bomb drop. Oh, irreverence in a reverent setting. It has the power to tickle us all, except the utterly humorless and self-absorbed.]

MINDY: I want to suggest to you, right now, that you are dead wrong. If you wanted it; if you applied yourself every day, no checking out, no giving up, to solving a problem, to change something you see not-working in this world—a glitch in its design, a horrifying injustice, an ugliness in people that should never have been nurtured to its full potential as hatred and violence in the first place—you CAN. I want to suggest that there is no problem so great it cannot be solved by a comprehensive, conscientious, crowd-sourced-and-edited, gut-checked and re-gut-checked and re-edited application of creativity and innovation; there is nothing that cannot be fixed with a better design.

Let's all ground ourselves in a few truths. Innovation itself causes brand new problems to be solved. The only constant in this world is change. But we can embrace that paradox like starving, sharp-clawed-and-attacking cuddly panda bear that it is. We can face this constant change and imbalance and conflict with total fearlessness, and get to Work. We can reshape all the negative patterns. We can put a full-stop to our self-fulfilling prophecies of shame and despair. We can repattern. We can reprophecize.

As Bruce Mau, with unabashed, bold, Helvetica confidence, posits, "we will create urban shelter for the entire world population." Density leads to efficiency! "We will enable sustainable mobility," by synthesizing energy, manufacturing, computing and materials. "We will bring energy to the entire world—sustainable energy…on a scale the world has never seen." We will get our Buckminster Fuller ON. "We will build a global mind…generating a worldwide cultural accumulation beyond imagination, available to anyone, anywhere." This, especially, will challenge us to come out of our self-shells, and share, and receive.

"We will make visible the as yet invisible," by using all the scientific apparatus at our current disposal and the to-be-invented to reveal all the information on the electromagnetic spectrum We will be able to see the smallest particles at the very center of all life, and the massive celestial objects swirling through the vast, glittering reaches of the galaxies.

Bruce is not finished with us. He believes "we will seamlessly integrate all supply and demand around the world." Yes! We will wrap our stubborn, inertia bound heads around brand new economic models that will generate ever more perfectly harmonized ecosystems. He also believes, "we will build intelligence in to the material and liberate them from matter." Bruce predicts that, "instead of designing a thing, we will design a designing thing." We will study the hardness and impenetrability of the diamond, the rapid growth of strong fibrous fungi; we will, "create superhero materials." He goes on to declare that, "we will eliminate the need for raw materials and banish waste." And we will not accomplish this by being recycling enthusiasts. No! We will accomplish this with design, by building intended reuse into every design in a constant, "never-ending loop of improvement."

Bruce then asks his only question. "Will we shift from the service of war to the service of life?" This is critical, we know, Bruce. We must redistribute our vast natural intellectual resources, stop applying them to the machines of war and greed, and reapply them to peace and stability and sustainability. He finishes with two big ones, resolving that, "we will design evolution and we will eradicate poverty," including poverty's children—chaos, heartbreak, mental strife, starvation and disease.

Guys! Listen! This means something important goddamnit! Everything counts! Everyone counts! Poets count. As professional engines of inspiration, remythologizers and cultural weavers, emotional spectrum decoders and healers; as inventors and designers of language, and masters of those tools that deftly tackle the problem of communicating about what words alone fail to adequately address—symbol and metaphor—we will not just be an integral part of this radical revolution in the design of the world. We just might be its leaders.

In the words of John Cage, "The world is getting better, s-l-o-w-l-y."[34-end] Let's speed it up. With our vast powers of understanding, translation, articulation and compassion. With our stories of survival and thriving against all odds. With our love. Our LOVE. LOVE. Let's go love ourselves, and love each other, and love this crazy world. Brave, fearless, radiant love. Love.

[Audience, professors and graduates and family and friends all leap to their feet in ovation. They are crying and smiling. They start turning to embrace one another.]

ASSIGNMENT

Pick one line or idea from this book that inspired you to action, or to see something differently—"develop new obsessions," "wield your vocabulary," "history is happening right now," "talk to your memories," *whatever*. Make a sign out of it, then go post that sign in a public place. Spread the word.

IN CONCLUSION

"I am a real rebel with a cause."
—Nina Simone

"All the lyrics to Stereolab's song 'Motoroller Scalatron.'"
—from their album Emperor Tomato Ketchup

Suspicions, Skeletons and Zebras—
A Bloody, Glittery Dénouement

When I was asked to write this book, I said "yes" only because the thought of it absolutely terrified me. I am in the purposeful habit, as you now know too well, of confronting what scares me. I stare it down with total irrational bravado; I am a Chihuahua barking up at a Neapolitan Mastiff. I bite off more than I can chew. I get in WAY over my head and flail about a lot until I figure out how to swim. It's how I learn.

Once it hit me that I had said "yes," I thought, "Oh fuck, what have I done?" I thought, "Who am I to teach anyone anything? I am so unripe! I'm still baking for chrissake!" I thought, "Writing poetry, whether I am 'good' at it or not is second nature to me now, and third and forth. How can I possibly articulate what I know? I don't even remember learning it. How can you teach what you don't remember learning?" And the moment I asked myself those rhetorical, self-doubting questions, my brain went to work at answering them, though I was unaware at a conscious level of its steady worrying at the task.

Memories arrived, slowly but surely, of my last twenty years (or twenty-six if you count that awkward jump start in the second grade), of how I learned to write poems, of who I learned it from and under what circumstances. So maybe I did have some remembered lessons to pass on. But I still felt I could not pass them on arbitrarily, not without "the cloud of context and possibility" that surrounded each move, each epiphany, each poem.

I also felt that I could not ask you to do what I was not willing to do myself. That *that* just wouldn't work. And I felt that if the best writing was in the business of showing-not-telling, then even if I was doing the work along with you, I could not tell you how I wrote without also trying, most sincerely, to show you. Guard down. Wizard-curtain-dropped. Dream-of-being-naked-at-school-exposed. And that's what I am now, on the other side of writing this book. Exposed.

I've never been much of an exhibitionist before. Not without the cloak of metaphor. Not without a stage, a microphone, and the explicit voyeuristic permission of an audience that knows why it's there and has come, at least to some degree, willingly. On purpose. To see the SHOW. Deep down, I am just an extrovert using smoke and mirrors and smile flash and all the distracting charms at my disposal to hide and protect my introvert, my private interior world where I can dream and think and imagine in total undisturbed serenity. It is the one place I am truly free.

I became a poet, it's possible, because I grew up in poverty, and writing is the cheapest art to practice besides humming. Or maybe because it was in me all along, a million seeds in my preacher DNA, nurtured to maturity by circumstance. Maybe I have been poetry's bitch my whole life, whether I knew it or not. Well, I know it now. However I arrived at this point, I belong to it now, poetry, and it belongs to me. I *need* it like I need sleep and food and breath, and it needs me. I cannot undo how it has shaped me, who I have become, who I am becoming because of it. But I am no longer afraid of what that means.

And now, you might want to go grab yourself a lake of fresh water because it's giant land-mass-in-Asia grain-of-salt time. (Cue the klaxons? Where *is* that klaxon flunky?) I am going to address something I said I would address WAY back at the chapter titled The Source. Ahem:

Everything I wrote in this book is *my* opinion. (Except, of course, where I stole the opinions of others with acknowledgement.) You should get very suspicious, if you are not already, of everything you just read. It is not pure fallen poetry-advice snow. It is so blackened and muddied with bias, you may as well be trudging the sidewalks to Grand Central Station in a Manhattan winter. Two main points:

Point #1: If you thought at any point while reading this book, "Of course she would say that. She's a blonde-haired blue-eyed white woman from Iowa, of all places. She has a college degree. She is the soul of American privilege," you were RIGHT. All of my opinions and ideas about writing and life and the world have grown directly from the decapitated-medusa-head of my experiences. These experiences shaped my perspective, which is—as is yours—biased, and mine is not just steeped in standard issue privilege, but something much worse, and much better—dumb luck. I was lucky to be born not how I *look*, but with the genetic gift of intelligence. Because of that, when I was a child I was given extra attention by intelligent adults. This special attention assured I got a good education in the public school system. I have also escaped accidental major head injuries in my thirty-plus years (knocks on all available wood), any serious consequences from my adolescent rebellions, many of which could have landed me in long-term incarceration, and any chronic and incurable diseases: DUMB LUCK.

Furthermore, I was born with some sort of built-in resilience-programming in me, some serious *bounce*. I was born with a personality bent towards optimism. These are inequities that don't often get acknowledged—that some of us are born not in to money, or status, but much richer riches: a greater capacity for joy, an inability to sustain anger and despair for long periods of time, a natural fearlessness, grit and determination. Some of us also come preset with an instinct to fight, rather than freeze or run, when danger approaches, even if it is just the danger of the Big Unknown, threatening to swallow us whole.

And some of us were born to parents who loved us and cherished us, even if it was short-lived, or even if the vibrations of that love were fighting to pass through the dense walls of love-distorting dysfunction. That love is also an inheritance, a great privilege, that not all of us are lucky enough to get. My parents loved me; they love me. It gives me more strength and comfort than I can describe. It will buoy me long after they are gone. Their love for me is my greatest unearned privilege.

Point #2: If at any point reading this book, you scoffed, had sharp witty criticisms arise and better ideas arise, that is fantastic. You should go forth doing what YOU want to do with your work as a poet. You should not give a cuss what I think, what Joan Jett thinks, what your professors and parents and friends and writing peers--well, you get it. You should invent and reinvent your philosophy and process as often as is necessary or as often as it just delights you to do so. There are no rules. We are ALL making this up as we go along.

All I ask is that you do whatever it is you do in your writing with all the bravery and moxy you can muster. What I am challenging—practically begging—you to do is abandon writing poetry as a purely intellectual exercise. Write poems that mean something to you, something fiercely personal, something that comes from the source that is you in all your you-ness. I want pieces of you to come out of hiding; I want your shadow selves to be allowed to play in the full light of consciousness. I want you to write what scares you and horrifies you with its truth, what elates you and tickles you with its absurdity and eccentricity, what nags at you with confusing emotion or with clear irony and with persistent, nightmarish emotional charge.

On that note, my final story:

My recurring nightmare as a child was about a skeleton. In the dream, I was in a long room, which was the floor of a house with many floors, and at each end of the room was a door. There was a skeleton magnetized to my feet, upside-down and "standing" on the ceiling that was the underside of the floor I was standing on. I could feel it beneath me. It was going to kill me, and I was terrified. I would run from one end of the room to the other, but when I arrived at the door it was there, me looking down at it, it bending up to look me in the face with its not-face, with its hollow bone eyes of death. I would scream in terror and run the other direction, to the other door, but it was always there. Attached to me, my inverted shadow. I could not escape.

I had that dream a hundred times at least, and would wake up in mortal panic and run to my mother's bed, where for a time, when I was smaller, she would let me in and I would be able to fall back asleep under her protection. Eventually, though, she could no longer take it—she needed her sleep—and would reject me, and send me back to my own bed to face my nightmares alone. Because of that dream, I have always been scared of skeletons—real ones, others and my own, the one I could feel (but generally refuse to) if I run two fingers up another finger, base to knuckle.

One psychologist, two Zen masters and a handful of mystics have speculated as to this dream's meaning, as our recurring nightmares as children are said to have great insight into our true natures, or our path to enlightenment that is, by necessity, our place of greatest difficulty. I've been told it might mean my greatest fear is of fear. (Really? So I'm, what, the spiritual reincarnation of FDR's greatest speech?) I have been told that it meant I would be blessed and cursed and dogged my whole life by the most powerful teacher there is—Death, its specter always near, reminding me that my life is a gift not to be taken for granted. I've also been told it means I am a doula, whose mission is to attend and facilitate the transitions into life (birth) and back out of it (death). I've been offered many insights. None of them softened my sharp, primal anxiety about the skeleton, the bone cage of its ribs grinning with the horror of no heart.

And then I saw the cover art designed for this book: a zebra with golden glitter stripes. The zebra had always represented something of the boring, oppressive black-and-white mindset to me. Its stripes suggested prison bars and implied something primal and triggering—an externalized skeletal ribcage. Seeing those stripes transformed into golden glitter--it freed me from something old. Something that maybe I didn't need anymore.

I have always *loved* the idea of power animals but, following my ethos of not "believing in" anything any more than I "don't-believe" in it, I relegated the idea to being some charming artifact of New-Ageism, or some not-so-charming co-opting of Native American cultural beliefs. But seeing the cover art, I went straight to Google, typed in "zebra power animal," clicked the I'm Feeling Lucky button, and was delivered to the appropriate page on a website, www.ShamanicJourney.com, which I will now just get straight to quoting directly, with some cuts and minor paraphrasing:

> The zebra's gifts include seeing in black and white, clarity without filters, balance, agility, uniqueness, power, sureness of path, keeping up individuality within the herd. The zebra's black and white stripes camouflage it against predators, who often can't identify individuals in the herd. However, to the herd members the patterns are [obviously different]…helping to identify one another, unique as our fingerprints. Blending into a crowd without losing your individuality is one powerful aspect of Zebra. Zebras also help us to be supportive members within our communities.
>
> The [zebra's] stripes represent the blending and balancing of opposites, yin yang, harmony - enabling us to see a deeper truth. If this is your power animal, study its ability to survive and flourish in a harsh land…Zebras enjoy challenge as they know that all challenges are a chance for growth. Use your mental ability to work around problems and barriers - Zebra will show you how.
>
> Questioning reality and illusion is common amongst people with zebra medicine…. The zebras pattern of black on white, or white on black implies that what you see is not always what you get. Zebras are master magicians, who utilize the energy of light and dark to shift realities and expand our consciousness, helping us see past our preconceived beliefs as they lead us into the mystery and magic of the unseen. Zebras seek balance in what they do, and they are sure of themselves, standing confidently in the middle of opposing forces. When the zebra comes into your life, change is imminent and hidden knowledge will be uncovered. Stand strong, develop trust and simply flow with the rhythm of a new creation.[35]

Whoa, Ina Woolcott from ShamanicJourney.com. Really glad I waited until the end of writing this book to look up that zebra-power-animal stuff. Knowing it was my cover art, I might have seriously crumbled under the spiritual pressure of living up to "Zebra Medicine." Bullet dodged.

So! Readers-who-have-made-it-to-the-end. I now bequeath to you all of the powers Ina described, but am adding golden sparkly party joy glitter. I am adding the gold that is the goal of all alchemy, and the glitter that is the spark, the inspiration, to take things to the next level and the next and the next, getting ever more meta, having more intense yes-fun with every connected burst of insight.

Let it now be declared that our new collective power animal is one that isn't "real"—the animal of the imagination. Let's go beyond the black and white clarity of what IS. Let's invent what isn't, what could be. Let's go way past balancing the opposites. Let's dive deep into the well in between them. Let's go past Nagwal. Let's go Nagual. (Look it up! Meso-America represent!)

Go—

be Brave!

WRITE.

Transform.

An Incomplete Poet's Dictionary, In Sweet, Conceptually-Jumbled, Alphabetical Order

Abstract object: An object which does not exist at any particular time or place, but rather exists as a type of thing (as an idea or abstraction), an important distinction in Philosophy.

Acrostic: A form of short verse constructed by placing a capitalized word or phrase vertically down the page to form the initial letters of each line of poetry. Each line is used to relate to the word, or praise the subject.

Adjective: A word that describes something (a noun), such as big, cold, or silly. One special type of adjective is an article, a word that introduces a noun and also limits or clarifies it; in English, the indefinite articles are 'a' and 'an'; the definite article is 'the.'

Adverb: A word that tells "how," "when," "where," or "how much." They almost always end in "ly," but not always, and examples include: easily, warmly, quickly, mainly, freely, and often.

Allegory: A symbolic narrative in which the surface details imply a secondary meaning. Allegory often takes the form of a story in which the characters represent moral qualities.

Alliteration: The repetition of consonant sounds, especially at the beginning of words.

Anapest: Two unaccented syllables followed by an accented one, as in com-pre-HEND or in-ter-VENE.

Antagonist: A character or force against which another character struggles.

Arc: The dramatic structure of a narrative. In Gustav Freytag's analysis of classic dramatic arc, a drama is divided into five parts, or acts: exposition, rising action, climax, falling action, and dénouement.

Arrangement: The order (or reordering) of words, or of phrases, or of stanzas in a poem.

Assonance: The repetition of similar vowel sounds.

Aubade: A tortured love lyric.

Ballad: A narrative poem written in four-line stanzas, characterized by swift action and narrated in a direct style.

Blank Verse: A line of poetry or prose in unrhymed iambic pentameter.

Caesura: A strong pause within a line of verse.

Canzone: A lyric poem of varying line length and metrical patterns.

Capitonym: A word that changes its meaning (and sometimes pronunciation) when it is capitalized, and usually applies to capitalization due to proper nouns or eponyms.

Character: An "imaginary person" that inhabits a literary work. Literary characters may be major or minor, static (unchanging) or dynamic (capable of change).

Characterization: The means by which writers present and reveal character. Although techniques of characterization are complex, writers typically reveal characters through their speech, dress, manner, and actions.

Choka: A Japanese Long Poem form consisting of a series of Katuata joined together, which gives a choice of form structures. The form evolved to introduce the Japanese equivalent of a couplet consisting of 12 onji, or sound units, pausing after the fifth unit, giving it a structured sequence of multiples of 5 - 7 onji and still with a finishing sequence using the Katuata of 5 - 7 - 7 (19) onji, or 5 - 7 - 5 (17) onji.

Chronological: The arrangement of events in the order of their occurrence.

Cinquain: A five-line stanza form with a specific syllable count starting with a two syllable line, and followed by three lines which increase by two syllables each time and the final line reverting to a two-syllable line again. In addition, the lines are usually iambic.

Clerihew: This form is a dipodic quatrain and consists of two rhymes: a. a. b. b. The title is the name of the person to be satirized, and is also the first line. (I included this form just because I like its name.)

Closed form: A type of form or structure in poetry characterized by regularity and consistency in such elements as rhyme, line length, and metrical pattern.

Complication: An intensification of the conflict in a story or play. Complication builds up, accumulates, and develops the primary or central conflict in a literary work.

Concrete object: In physics, a physical body or physical object. In poetry, any object that is real and exists and is not alive; it cannot get up and walk away on its own.

Conflict: A struggle between opposing forces in a story, typically resolved or left intentionally unresolved by the end of the work.

Conjunction: Any member of a small class of words distinguished in many languages by their function as connectors between words, phrases, clauses, or sentences, such as: and, because, but, however.

Connotation: The associations called up by a word that goes beyond its dictionary meaning.

Contraction: A shortened form of a word or group of words, with the omitted letters often replaced in written English by an apostrophe; for example: e'er for ever, isn't for is not, dep't for department.

Convention: A customary feature of a literary work, such as the use of a chorus in Greek tragedy, the inclusion of an explicit moral in a fable, or the use of a particular rhyme scheme in a villanelle.

Couplet: A pair of rhymed lines that may or may not constitute a separate stanza in a poem, though in modern poetry rhyme is not necessary for two lines to be referred to as a couplet.

Dactyl: A stressed syllable followed by two unstressed ones, as in FLUT-ter-ing or BLUE-ber-ry.

Denotation: The dictionary meaning of a word. Writers typically play off a word's denotative meaning against its connotations, or suggested and implied associational implications.

Denouement: Also referred to as resolution: the sorting out or unraveling of a plot at the end.

Dialogue: The conversation of characters in a literary work. In fiction and poetry, dialogue is typically enclosed within quotation marks, but in poetry it is sometimes indicated instead with italics.

Diction: The selection of words in a literary work. A work's diction forms one of its centrally important literary elements, as writers use words to convey action, reveal character, imply attitudes, identify themes and suggest values.

Elegy: A lyric poem that laments the dead.

Elision: The omission of an unstressed vowel or syllable to preserve the meter of a line of poetry.

Enjambment: A run-on line of poetry in which logical and grammatical sense carries over from one line into the next. An enjambed line differs from an end-stopped line in which the grammatical and logical sense is completed within the line.

Epic: Traditionally a long narrative poem that records the adventures of a hero, but in modern times can be used to simply describe a poem of great length and breadth.

Epigram: A brief, witty poem, often satirical.

Epigraph: A short quotation or saying at the beginning of a book or chapter, intended to suggest its theme.

Eponym: A word based on or derived from a person's name.

Exposition: Anywhere in a piece in which necessary background information is provided.

Falling action: The action following the climax of the work that moves it towards its denouement or resolution.

Falling meter: Poetic meters such as trochaic and dactylic that move or fall from a stressed to an unstressed syllable.

Fiction: An imagined story, whether in prose, poetry, or drama.

Figurative language: A form of language use in which writers and speakers convey something other than the literal meaning of their words. Examples include hyperbole or exaggeration, litotes or understatement, simile and metaphor, which employ comparison, and synecdoche and metonymy, in which a part of a thing stands for the whole.

Flashback: An interruption of a work's chronology to describe or present an incident that occurred prior to the main time frame of a work's action. Writers use flashbacks to complicate the sense of chronology in the plot of their works and to convey the richness of the experience of human time.

Foil: A character who contrasts and parallels the main character in a play or story.

Foot: A metrical unit composed of stressed and unstressed syllables.

Foreshadowing: Hints of what is to come.

Free verse: Poetry without a regular pattern of meter or rhyme. The verse is "free" in not being bound by earlier poetic conventions requiring poems to adhere to an explicit and identifiable meter and rhyme scheme in a form such as the sonnet or ballad. Modern and contemporary poets of the twentieth and twenty-first centuries often employ free verse.

Ghazal: A series of couplets, each one capable of standing alone as a poem. The first couplet is called the matla or the place where the heavenly body rises. This couplet also sets the meter of the poems and the rhyming pattern. In the true Ghazal, the last word/s of both lines of the first couplet must be the same and, similarly, the last line of the following couplets must also end with the same word/s. Modern Ghazals seem only to rhyme these last words.

Gothic: A style usually portraying fantastic tales dealing with horror, despair, the grotesque and other "dark" subjects.

Haiku: A Japanese poem of seventeen syllables, in three lines of 5, 7, and 5.

Heteronym: A word spelled the same as another but having a different sound and meaning, as lead (to conduct) and lead (a metal).

Homonym: A word that is the same as another in sound and spelling, but different in meaning, as chase "to pursue" and chase "to ornament metal."

Homograph: A word of the same written form as another but of different meaning and, usually, origin, whether pronounced the same way or not, as bear 1 "to carry; support" and bear 2 "animal" or lead 1 "to conduct" and lead 2 "metal."

Homophone: A word pronounced the same as another but differing in meaning, whether spelled the same way or not, as in heir and air.

Hyperbole: A figure of speech involving exaggeration.

Iamb: An unstressed syllable followed by a stressed one, as in to-DAY.

Image: A concrete representation of a sense impression, a feeling, or an idea. In some works one image predominates either by recurring throughout the work or by appearing at a critical point. Often writers use multiple images throughout a work to suggest states of feeling and to convey implications of thought and action. Some modern poets, such as Ezra Pound and William Carlos Williams, write poems that lack discursive explanation entirely and include only images.

Imagery: The pattern of related comparative aspects of language, particularly of images, in a literary work.

Interjection: Any member of a class of words expressing emotion, distinguished in most languages by their use in grammatical isolation, as Hey! Oh! Ouch! Ugh! Also, any other word or expression so used, as Good grief! or Indeed!

Internal Rhyme: A rhyme created by two or more words in the same line of verse.

Irony: A contrast or discrepancy between what is said and what is meant, or between what happens and what is expected to happen in life and in literature. In verbal irony, characters say the opposite of what they mean. In irony of circumstance or situation, the opposite of what is expected occurs. In dramatic irony, a character speaks in ignorance of a situation or event known to the reader or to the audience or to the other characters.

Katuata: A Japanese poem form consisting of 19 sound units or onji (in the west we would describe this as having a syllable count of 19), with a break after the fifth and twelfth onji and this would give us a form structure of. 5 - 7 - 7. (It's not a haiku! Try it!)

Lai and Virelai: A poem form that consists of five syllabled couplets followed by a two-syllable line. The number of lines in each stanza is fixed at nine and the couplets must rhyme with each other, as the two syllable lines must also rhyme. The Lai is a very old French form and tradition states that the short line must not be indented, it must be left dressed to the poem. This is known as Arbre Fourchu (Forked Tree) because there is a pattern meant to be set up as a tree.

Limerick: A popular rhyming poem form with two options: a five-line stanza, or a four-line form. Traditionally, the first and fifth lines ended in the same word.

Literal language: A form of language in which writers and speakers mean exactly what their words denote.

Luc Bat: A Vietnamese form of poetry, which simply means six eight. The odd lines (1, 3, 5, etc.) are six sound units and the even lines (2, 4, 6, etc.) are eight sound units long, hence the title. The rhyming scheme is simple, also. The last word (sixth sound unit) of the odd lines rhymes with the sixth sound unit of the even lines, and the eighth sound unit rhymes with the sixth unit of the next odd line. The final even line links back to the first line.

Lyric poem: A type of poem characterized by brevity, compression, and the expression of feeling.

Mathnawi: A poem form written in rhyming couplets, believed to have emerged from an Iranian form around the 4th - 10th century. The subject is usually heroic, romantic, or religious, and some Persian Mathnawi are especially significant in Sufism.

Mawaddes: An ancient Ethiopian ecclesiastic verse form that was adopted into the western liturgical world. Mawaddes are often recited after Vespers at "first cock crow," before Matins. The mono-rhymed form has also crossed over into the secular world. It contains 9 lines. They may be metered, Alexandrine lines, iambic hexameter lines with midline caesura or monorhymes. They must have religious or secular overtones, as the the form is intended to capture the "sacred."

Metaphor: A comparison between essentially unlike things without an explicitly comparative word such as like or as. Also: the foundation and building blocks of all great poetry.

Meter: The measured pattern of rhythmic accents in poems.

Metonymy: A figure of speech in which a closely related term is substituted for an object or idea.

Mood: The collective descriptors that induce or suggest a particular feeling or state of mind.

Narrative poem: A poem that tells a story.

Narrator: The voice and implied speaker of a fictional work, to be distinguished from the actual living author.

Noun: A type of word that represents a person, thing, or place.

Octave: Any eight-line poetry form. Also, significantly, a series of eight notes occupying the interval between two notes, one having twice or half the frequency of vibration of the other: A-B-C-D-E-F-G-A on the piano.

Ode: A long, stately poem praising its subject. Sometimes a serious poem on an exalted subject, such as Horace's "Eheu fugaces," but sometimes a more lighthearted work, such as Neruda's "Ode to My Socks."

Onomatopoeia: The use of words to imitate the sounds they describe. Words such as buzz and crack are onomatopoetic.

Open form: A type of structure or form in poetry characterized by freedom from regularity and consistency in such elements as rhyme, line length, metrical pattern, and overall poetic structure. AKA, E.E. Cummings's style.

Pantoum: Originally a Malaysian form of poetry, it was adopted and adapted by the French and became very popular with them. The rhyme pattern is as follows; A1, B1, A2, B2, ... B1, C1, B2, C2, etc., the last stanza being Z1, A2, Z2, A1 (note the reversal of the final repeat couplet thus completing the circle). Unlike most of these strict repeating forms, if we retain the original Malaysian format, there is no set stanza count, syllable count, or need for the last stanza to repeat back to the first. This makes the Pantoum ideal for narratives that demand repetition or emphasis.

Parody: A humorous, mocking imitation of a literary work, sometimes sarcastic, but often playful and even respectful in its playful imitation.

Persona Poem: A poem written from the point-of-view of the object or person being written about. Also referred to as "mask poems."

Personification: The endowment of inanimate objects or abstract concepts with animate or living qualities.

Pleiades: This is a very new form. The Pleiades form was invented in 1999 by Craig Tigerman, Sol Magazine's Lead Editor. The Pleiades is a star cluster in the Taurus constellation discovered by the Greeks and named after the Seven Sisters, Alcyone, Asterope, Celaeno, Electra, Maia, Merope, and Tygeta. The basic form consists of seven lines, each line starting with the same letter as the one word title, and at first no meter or syllable count was specified.

Plot: The unified structure of incidents in a literary work.

Point of view: The angle of vision from which a story is narrated. A work's point of view can be: first person, in which the narrator is a character or an observer, respectively; objective, in which the narrator knows or appears to know no more than the reader; omniscient, in which the narrator knows everything about the characters; and limited omniscient, which allows the narrator to know some things about the characters, but not everything. A point of view can be executed in 1st person ("I saw"), 2nd person ("You saw"), 3rd person ("She/He/They saw"), all available in singular or plural forms.

Portmanteau: A combination of two (or more) words or morphemes into one new word.

Praise Poetry: A form that is commonly found specifically in South African nations (though certainly forms of praise poetry are found everywhere, like the Ode), and is a popular indigenous oral tradition which, in the past century, has transitioned to the literary world. In Zulu it is called izibongo, Lesotho dithoko, and in Setswana, maboko. The poetry celebrates national heroes and kings and is more laudatory than epic. It doesn't tell a story; it simply lavishes praise on the subject. They were composed often right after a personal or national victory, or for gatherings of various kinds. They seem to be the counterpart to Insult Poetry.

Preposition: A word that shows how something is related to another word. It shows the spatial (space), temporal (time), or logical relationship of an object to the rest of the sentence. The words above, near, at, by, after, with and from are prepositions.

Pronoun: A substitute for a noun. Some pronouns are: I, me, she, hers, he, him, it, you, they, them, etc.

Quatrain: A four-line stanza in a poem.

Recognition: The point at which a character understands his or her situation as it really is.

Reversal: The point at which the action of the plot turns in an unexpected direction, also commonly referred to as the "turn."

Rhyme: The matching of final vowel or consonant sounds in two or more words.

Rhythm: The recurrence of accent or stress in lines of verse.

Rising action: A set of conflicts and crises that constitute the part of a story's plot leading up to the climax.

Rising meter: Poetic meters such as iambic and anapestic that move or ascend from an unstressed to a stressed syllable.

Rondeau: A very underestimated and sometimes a very challenging poetry form. It consists of three stanzas, a quintet (5 lines), a quatrain (4 lines) and a sestet (6 lines), giving a total of 15 lines. The first phrase of the first line usually sets the refrain R; it is admissible to use the whole line as the refrain. The rhyme scheme is: R. a. a. b. b. a .... a. a. b. R. .... a. a. b. b. a. R. The meter is considered be open, and the French style is not bound by a rhyming pattern and is also more of a light and buoyant, even "flashy" form of poetry which uses short lines. The English style, however, is much more dour and serious, even meditative, and uses tetrameter or pentameter.

Rondel: Another beautiful but neglected poetry form having lost its popularity to others in the passage of fashions. Basically, it's a 13-line poem which forms around two rhymes. There is a refrain, which is set up by the first two lines of the first stanza. The rhyme pattern is A. B. a. b. and .a. b. A. B. for the first two stanzas, and a quintain for the final stanza that mirrors the first two stanzas, with the last line repeating the first line of the first stanza: a. b. b. a. A.

Rondo: A musical form with a recurring leading theme, often found in the final movement of a sonata or concerto.

Rophalic Verse: A very deceptive form that, at first, appears simple, but in fact it requires a lot of hard work to accomplish a satisfactory piece. The rules are simple; with each line, the first word is monosyllabic, the second word has two syllables, the third three syllables, and so on.

Satire: A literary work that criticizes human misconduct and ridicules vices, stupidities, and follies.

Sestina: A poem of thirty-nine lines written in iambic pentameter. Its six-line stanzas repeat in an intricate and prescribed order the final word in each of the first six lines. After the sixth stanza, there is a three-line envoi, which uses the six repeating words, two per line.

Setting: The time and place of a literary work which establish its context.

Sijo: Like the Haiku, the traditional Sijo is a three line poem, but there the similarity ends. Unlike the Haiku, the Sijo can have any number of stanzas to make it a ballad or a lyric, and it can contain metaphor and other similar ideas. The traditional Sijo is about 44 syllables consisting of four phrase groups per line. It is usually broken up this way: 3. 4. 3. 4./ 3. 4. 3. 4./ 3. 6. 4. 3.

Simile: A figure of speech involving a comparison between unlike things using like, as, or as though.

Sonnet: A fourteen-line poem in iambic pentameter. The Shakespearean or English sonnet is arranged as three quatrains and a final couplet, rhyming abab cdcd efef gg. The Petrarchan or Italian sonnet divides into two parts: an eight-line octave and a six-line sestet, rhyming abba abba cde cde or abba abba cd cd cd. There are too many types of sonnets to describe here.

Spondee: A metrical foot represented by two stressed syllables, such as KNICK-KNACK.

Stanza: A division or unit of a poem that is repeated in the same form—either with similar or identical patterns or rhyme and meter, or with variations from one stanza to another.

Style: The way an author chooses words, arranges them in sentences or in lines of dialogue or verse, and develops ideas and actions with description, imagery, and other literary techniques.

Subject: What a story or sentence is about; to be distinguished from plot and theme, or other nouns or pronouns in the sentence.

Subplot: A subsidiary or subordinate or parallel plot in a play or story that coexists with the main plot.

Symbol: An object or action in a literary work that means more than itself, that stands for something beyond itself.

Synecdoche: A figure of speech in which a part is substituted for the whole.

Synesthesia: The production of a sense impression relating to one sense or part of the body by stimulation of another sense or part of the body. Also, the poetic description of a sense impression in terms of another sense, as in "a loud perfume."

Syntax: The grammatical order of words in a sentence or line of verse or dialogue. The organization of words and phrases and clauses in sentences of prose, verse and dialogue. In the following example, normal syntax (subject, verb, object order) is inverted: "Whose woods these are I think I know."

Tanka: The original pattern of Tanka (a short poem) established centuries ago was a length of about twelve onji or sound-units, pausing after the fifth and seventh onji. Two twelve-unit segments were joined, with the closure a final seven-sound phrase added. This means that a Tanka has three parts, and each one is capable of standing alone. This created the classic 5 - 7 - 5 - 7 - 7 Tanka.

Tercet: A three-line stanza, as the stanzas in Frost's "Acquainted With the Night" and Shelley's "Ode to the West Wind." The three-line stanzas or sections that, together, constitute the sestet of a Petrarchan or Italian sonnet.

Terza Rima: A challenging poetry form of Italian origin. In the original form, there was no set meter, although it is normal to keep a constant syllable count and line length. In the modern version, the syllables are accentuated and usually iambic tetrameter or pentameter. Lines 1 and 3 rhyme with each other, and line 2 sets the rhyme for the next stanza. There can be any number of tercets, or three-line stanzas, and it is a matter of preference whether you link back to the first stanza or not. If there is no link back, it's normal to terminate with a couplet that rhymes with the previous stanza. The rhyme patterns are ....a. b. a...b. c. b... c. d. c. etc., finishing x. a. x. or x. x. etc.

Theme: The idea of a literary work abstracted from its details of language, character, and action, and cast in the form of a generalization.

Tone: The implied attitude of a writer toward the subject and characters of a work.

Trochee: An accented syllable followed by an unaccented one, as in FOOT-ball.

Typography: The general character or appearance of printed matter, i.e. capitalization, italics.

Understatement: A figure of speech in which a writer or speaker says less than what he or she means; the opposite of exaggeration.

Verb: A type of word that describes an action or a state of being. Types of verbs include normal verbs (to touch); non-continuous verbs types like abstract verbs (to seem), possession verbs (to belong), emotion verbs (to envy); and mixed-verbs.

Villanelle: A nineteen-line lyric poem that relies heavily on repetition. The first and third lines alternate throughout the poem, which is structured in six stanzas—five tercets and a concluding quatrain.

Zebra: A poem whose entire usage of device and form is exceptional at revealing and explicating hidden, complicated truths beyond that black-and-white; the truth that lies in between. (I just made that one up.)

References

1— from Bruce Mau's *An Incomplete Manifesto for Growth*. Also, for kicks, see "Maunifesto" on www.textism.com, author unknown at time of publication.

2—Rob Brezsny, *PRONOIA Is the Antidote for Paranoia: How the Whole World Is Conspiring to Shower You with Blessings*

3—Carolyn Kaufman, *Three-Dimensional Villains: Finding Your Character's Shadow*

4—"Poet Kay Ryan: A profile," by Elizabeth Lund, *The Christian Science Monitor*, August 25, 2004

5—James Wanless, PH.D., *The Voyager Tarot Guidebook*, pg. 1

6—Alan Moore, *Promethea*

7—Jack Hirschman, "Path"

8—Natalie Goldberg, *Writing Down The Bones—Freeing The Writer Within*, pg. 8

9—Joseph Campbell, *The Hero with a Thousand Faces*

10— Eckhart Tolle, *The Power of Now*

11—Bob Hicock, "Backward Poem"

12—Rachel McKibbens, in general: www.rachelmckibbens.com

13—Carl Sagan, *Contact*, and also, well, in general.

14—RadioLab, WNYC, produced by Jad Abumrad and Robert Krulwich, Season 8, Episode 2: *Words*

15—http://manonwire.com/

16—from "Guard Duty," by Tomas Tranströmer, translated by Robert Bly in *The Finished Heaven*, Greywolf Press, 2001

17—Robert Bly, "Upward Into The Depths," an introduction to *The Finished Heaven* (see 16)

18—This American Life, Episode 405: *Inside Job*

19—Susan Adams, "Board Changes At BATS And Goldman Sachs Not Nearly Enough," www.forbes.com

20—post by Levi Sumagaysay, "Quoted: on Goldman Sachs op-ed," Good Morning Silicon Valley, blogs.siliconvalley.com

21—Hamilton Nolan, "You Are Not Going to Win the Lottery, You Fool," www.gawker.com

22—Rebecca Solnit, "Men Explain Things to Me/Facts Didn't Get in Their Way," found at www.tomdispatch.com, a project of The Nation Institute

23—Wikipedia entry on Gestalt Therapy, in the section Phenomenological Method in March, 2012.

24—Elizabeth Scott, M.S. ,"Cortisol and Stress: How to Stay Healthy," published on www.about.com

25—Hans Verlinde, PhD, "Is Each Snowflake Unique," Probing Questions Blog on the ResearchPennState website www.rps.psu.edu, production of Penn State University.

26—Anthony Zador, PhD, "Scientists At Cold Spring Harbor Laboratory Make Progress In Determining How The Brain Selectively Interprets Sound," interviewed in the Cold Spring Harbor Laboratory (CSHL) news and features section of their website www.cshl.edu , referencing "Sparse Representation of Sounds in the Unanesthetized Auditory Cortex" which appears in Public Library of Science: Biology on January 28. The compete citation is as follows: Tomáš Hromádka, Michael R. DeWeese, Anthony M. Zador.

27—Feyza Sancar, "Music and the Brain: Processing and Responding (A General Overview)," published on Bryn Mawr College's website at www. serendip.brynmawr.edu

28—Joss Whedon, *Buffy the Vampire Slayer*

29— James Wanless, PH.D., *The Voyager Tarot Guidebook*, pg. 30

30—Chuck Wendig, "25 Things You Should Know About Creativity," http://terribleminds.com

31—Timothy Leary, *High Priest*, Trip 15 "Your Faith Will Perform Miracle: The Good Friday Experiment," pg. 317

32—Wikipedia entry on "Psilocybin mushroom."

33—Wikipedia entry on "Eight-circuit model of consciousness"

34—Bruce Mau, Jennifer Leonard and the Institute without Boundaries, *Massive Change, Bruce Mau and the Institute without Boundaries*, Phaidon Press

35—Ina Woolcott, "Zebra, Power Animal, Symbol of Individuality, Balance" from www.shamanicjourney.com

About the Author

Mindy Nettifee is the director of the nonprofit organization Write Now Poetry Society and the author of two full-length collections of poetry, *Sleepyhead Assassins* (Moon Tide Press) and *Rise of the Trust Fall* (Write Bloody Press). An alumna of Chapman Univeristy, she has taught poetry workshops at community centers, schools and universities across the country for 15 years and has curated poetry events for the Smithsonian Project, the Getty Center, the Los Angeles County Arts Commission and others. She is a cast member of the groundbreaking performance poetry tours The Last Nerve and The Whirlwind Company, and currently writes from the pine trees of Portland, Oregon. She can be reached for booking and other inquiries at www. thecultofmindy.com.

TEAR-OUT INSPIRADO

That's what most of us want in the end, after all. That's why we're writing. We want someone to understand us, to see us.

To get us.

If we could say what we're trying to say any other way, we wouldn't have to write the poems.

If you're not afraid of those hidden inner clockworks, of what you'll find in the dark, you're not paying attention. But

bravery is not about lacking fear;

it's about being scared out of your mind and still taking the plunge.

How you do **anything** is how you do **everything.**

Imagine writing as a muscle that you need to use, maybe daily, but at least several times a week so that it gets stronger, so that more blood flows to it. **You need the blood flow.** If there is no blood flow, there can be no glitter.

I think it is truly beautiful
when humans, small
specks that we are,
attempt to and believe
we can understand
the whole.
I think writing poetry and
using metaphor to try to
understand or explain
the things we cannot talk
about directly, or have
no words for, is beautiful.

What makes me love a poem is not only that it has gorgeous language or daring implications or the **punch of wisdom;** it's that I feel like I have learned something about the writer.

I fall in love when I feel no one else could have written what I'm reading.

If you are terrified of writing about it,

if you're afraid of what it means that you feel this way, of what other people would think of you if you wrote about it, if you feel your ego resisting it with every nasty tool in its arsenal—put it on the list.

Resolve to

go there.

Be intentional about your meaning. Even when you don't exactly know what you mean.

Abandon writing poetry as a purely intellectual exercise. Write poems that mean something to you, something **fiercely personal**...

I want pieces of you to come out of hiding; I want your shadow selves to be allowed to play in the full light of consciousness. I want you to write what scares you and horrifies you with its truth, what elates you with its absurdity and eccentricity, what nags at you with confusing emotion or with clear irony and with

persistent, nightmarish emotional charge.

Onward to the cliffs!

IF YOU LIKE MINDY NETTIFEE,
MINDY NETTIFEE LIKES...

Everything Is Everything
Cristin O'Keefe Aptowicz

These Are the Breaks
Idris Goodwin

Birthday Girl with Possum
Brendan Constantine

Time Bomb Snooze Alarm
Bucky Sinister

The Undisputed Greatest Writer of All Time
Beau Sia

Want to know more about Write Bloody books, authors and events?
Join our maling list at:

www.writebloody.com

CPSIA information can be obtained
at www.ICGtesting.com
Printed in the USA
FSHW010753160519
58186FS

9 781938 912016